Father's House

Glimpses of the Glory

By Timothy J. E. Cross BA BD PGCE

MY FATHER'S HOUSE

First Published 1993

Ambassador Productions Ltd
Providence House
16 Hillview Avenue,
Belfast, BT5 6JR

ISBN 0 907927 88 2

FOREWORD

'Every Christian,' writes Timothy Cross, 'has a "homing instinct" for heaven,' and he is right. It ought to follow, then, that the more we know about heaven, this side, the better will be our preparation for it.

In making any journey, we need to be sure as to where we are going. Being wise means knowing that God is preparing us for another world where his light will shine on us as it never did in this one. Revelation 7:9-17 is meant as a heart-warming picture of heaven and tells us a great deal about the international community that is to be found there. It informs us not only who they are, but where they have come from, the means by which they came, and their present employment. Who would not want such glimpses of the glory, save those whose hearts are unprepared for heaven?

Timothy Cross has written a book in which he gives us 'glimpses of glory' - not merely to satisfy our mental curiosity, but as all good theology is meant to do, to warn our hearts and make us long for it ourselves. C. S. Lewis described heaven as a delight compared with which all the raptures of earthly lovers are mere milk and water! Timothy Cross has managed to unpack these verses in Revelation and give us a foretaste of the 'delight' that is in store for God's children.

It is a delight to read what he has written, and a privilege to commend his work. 'I see myself now at the end of my journey,' said Bunyan's Mr. Stand-fast, as he stood halfway into Jordan's water. 'The thoughts of what I am going to, and of the conduct that waits for me on the other side, doth lie as a glowing coal at my heart ... I have formerly lived by hearsay and faith, but now I go where I shall live by sight, and shall be with him in whose company I delight myself.' Such a 'glowing coal' is what this book is all about.

Derek Thomas
February, 1993

ABOUT THE AUTHOR

Timothy Cross was converted to Christ in his later teens and holds academic awards from the University of Wales at both undergraduate and postgraduate levels. Cardiff born, he now resides in Belfast, Northern Ireland, but can still be heard each month broadcasting the Gospel on the South Wales Talking Magazine for the blind. He lists long-distance running as his main hobby.

CONTENTS

After this I looked, and behold, a great multitude which no man could number from every nation, from all tribes and peoples and tongues, standing before the throne and before the Lamb, clothed in white robes, with palm branches in their hands, and crying out with a loud voice, "Salvation belongs to our God Who sits upon the throne, and to the Lamb!" And all the angels stood around the throne and round the elders and the four living creatures, and they fell on their faces before the throne and worshipped God, saying, "Amen! Blessing and glory and wisdom and thanksgiving and honour and power and might be to our God for ever and ever! Amen."

Then one of the elders addressed me, saying, "Who are these, clothed in white robes, and whence have they come?" I said to him, "Sir, you know." And he said to me, "These are they who have come out of the great tribulation; they have washed their robes and made them white in the blood of the Lamb.

Therefore are they before the throne of God,
and serve Him day and night within His temple;
and He Who sits upon the throne will shelter them with
    His presence.
They shall hunger no more, neither thirst any more;
the sun shall not strike them, nor any scorching heat.
For the Lamb in the midst of the throne will be their
    shepherd,
and He will guide them to springs of living water,
and God will wipe away every tear from their eyes."

INTRODUCTION

Surprisingly few books on heaven have been published in recent years. This book attempts to redress the
balance. Whilst heaven is predominantly the dwelling
place of Almighty God, it is also the eternal home of
those who have been saved by God's grace in Jesus
Christ. Every Christian, quite naturally, has a 'homing
instinct' for heaven, and this is reflected in the 'Life to
Come' sections of some hymn books, with sub-sections
such as 'Aspirations after heaven,' 'Heaven anticipated'
and 'The redeemed in heaven.' The Apostle Paul echoed
every true believer's yearning when he wrote *my desire
is to be with Christ, for that is far better* (Philippians 1:23),
just as King David had previously penned *In Thy
presence there is fullness of joy, in Thy right hand are
pleasures forever more.* (Psalm 16:11)

Whilst every Christian, by virtue of Christ's atoning
death, can enjoy a measure of God's presence now, even
in this life, heaven may be described as God's immediate presence, and the glories of this place just cannot be
told as *no eye has seen, nor ear heard nor the heart of
man conceived, what God has prepared for those who
love Him.* (1 Corinthians 2:9) Does this make such a
book as this pointless therefore? Yes and no! Yes, in that
the reality of heaven will always be more wonderful than
mere words can encapsulate. No in that the Bible, God's
written revelation gives us many glimpses of the Christian's glory to come. Whilst it is true that there is much
that we have not the capacity to understand now, it is
nevertheless incumbent upon the Christian to read, and
seek to understand what God Himself has revealed

concerning the glories of the heavenly life. *All Scripture is inspired by God and profitable* (2 Timothy 3:16).

The book of Revelation, as part of Holy Scripture is exceedingly *profitable*. This book gives us more glimpses of the glory to come than any other book in the inspired volume. Two thousand years ago, the Apostle John, exiled on the Isle of Patmos, was given the most remarkable vision of heaven. *After this I looked, and lo, in heaven an open door!* (4:1) Revelation is indeed revealing! Its name means 'the unveiling', and here we are not dealing with idle speculation but concrete reality, as it was God the Holy Spirit Who gave us the book of Revelation through His servant John. Revelation thus is as true as the God Who is ultimate truth; Jesus Himself promised that *When the Spirit of truth comes, He will guide you into all truth... and He will declare to you the things to come.* (John 16:13) And the God Who inspired Revelation has seen fit to preserve it for the encouragement and consolation of Christians today.

Let us now then explore some aspects of heaven, which God has revealed to us in His Book. This book is sent out with the twofold hope that 1. Christians whose lot in this world is anything but heavenly may be encouraged as they are reassured of God's sovereignty, love and the undefeatability of His purposes. 2. Any non-Christians whose curiosity may have been aroused will come to know Him Whose death on the Cross is the only way to heaven - as it is only by the blood of Jesus that we can be certain that our sins are forgiven, and we have peace with God both here and hereafter.

Timothy J. E. Cross
Belfast, N. Ireland
March, 1993

CHAPTER ONE

The Divine Scene of Heaven

After this I looked, and behold, a great multitude which no man could number, from every nation, from all tribes and peoples and tongues, standing before the throne and before the Lamb, clothed in white robes, with palm branches in their hands, and crying out with a loud voice, "Salvation belongs to our God Who sits upon the throne, and to the Lamb!" And all the angels stood round the throne and round the elders and the four living creatures, and they fell on their faces before the throne saying, "Amen! Blessing and glory and wisdom and thanksgiving and honour and power and might be to our God for ever and ever! Amen." (Revelation 7:9-12)

Here we are privileged to be given an insight into heaven itself and the activities going on there! By its very nature, we could never find out such inspired and inspiring information unless God had first graciously revealed it to us. Here then, we are not dealing with human speculation but Divine revelation. What do we glimpse here concerning the Divine scene of heaven? Notice five points:-

The Congregation, Consummation, Clothes, Conquest, Cry and Chorus.

1. THE CONGREGATION

i. They are a multitudious people

The redeemed in heaven are described here as being *a great multitude which no man can number*.(7:9) There we see the vastness of God's redeeming love! Remember that if God was strictly just, no one at all would enter heaven. God cannot abide sinners in His presence, yet *all have sinned and fall short of the glory of God* (Romans 3:23), and every one that has ever lived (Christ excepted) is *by nature children of wrath*. (Ephesians 2:3) It follows then, that the great multitude are only there in heaven because of God's mercy. He need not have saved any, but He chose to save some - He chose to save a great multitude! This multitude in heaven are there solely because of the grace of God - God the Father Who chose them; God the Son Who died for their sins and God the Holy Spirit Who brought them to saving faith in Christ. The multitude is evidence of the vastness of the love of the God Who *so loved the world that He gave His only Son that whoever believes in Him should not perish but have eternal life*. (John 3:16) It is this multitude which no man can number who are the fulfilment of God's promise to Abraham made four thousand years ago. *Look toward heaven and number the stars if you are able to number them. Then He said 'So shall your descendants be.' And he believed the Lord; and He reckoned it to him as righteousness.* (Genesis 15:5,6) True believers are the spiritual descendants of Abraham, the man who was justified by faith. *If you are Christ's then you are Abraham's offspring, heirs according to promise.* (Galatians 3:29)

ii. They are multinational people

The great multitude of heaven are described as hailing from *every nation, from all tribes and peoples and tongues*. (7:9) Here we glimpse something of the impartiality of God's love. An ugly fact of this world is discrimination and racism. Legislation attempts to eradicate this, but no legislation can legislate away the hatred, suspicion and hostility that lurks in the human heart between individuals and groups that differ. How good to know then, that God's love, whilst particular, is impartial and indiscriminate. We know this from the fact that in heaven the redeemed are *from every nation, from all tribes and peoples and tongues*.

In Old Testament times, God's saving activity was limited mainly to the nation of Israel - with some notable exceptions like Rahab and Ruth, two heathen women who joined the Covenant people of God. In Old Testament times, Israel apart, the nations were spiritually blinded and sunk in heathenism. Hints however are given in the Old Testament of better things to come. God prophesied of His Servant in Isaiah 49:6:- *It is too light a thing that You should be My servant to raise up the tribes of Jacob and to restore the preserved of Israel; I will give You as a light to the nations, that My salvation may reach to the ends of the earth*. This promise was fulfilled in Jesus, Whom Simeon extolled as *a light for revelation to the Gentiles and for glory to Thy people Israel*. (Luke 2:32) Jesus indeed is the light, not just of Israel but the whole world. He Himself stated *I am the light of the world. He who follows Me will not walk in darkness but will have the light of life*. (John 8:12)

It is this vast multinational multitude in heaven which proves the truth of the Bible's teaching on the imparti-

13

ality of the Divine grace. Peter preached *Truly I perceive that God shows no partiality but in every nation any one who fears Him and does what is right is acceptable to Him... everyone who believes in Him receives forgiveness of sins through His Name.* (Acts 10:34,43) And Paul taught *There is no distinction between Jew and Greek; the same Lord is Lord of all and bestows His riches upon all who call upon Him. For 'every one who calls upon the name of the Lord will be saved.'* (Romans 10:12,13) What a congregation! But notice secondly:-

2. THE CONSUMMATION

The multinational multitude of heaven are *standing before the throne and before the Lamb.* (Revelation 7:9) The Bible often describes heaven in terms of the blessed absence of certain things, for example *death shall be no more, neither shall there be mourning nor crying nor pain any more.* (Revelation 21:4) *There shall be no night there.* (Revelation 21:25) *There shall no more be anything accursed.* (Revelation 22:3) And whilst this will be gloriously true, for the Christian, what makes heaven heaven is not so much the welcome absence of suffering but the wonderful presence of God. In heaven we shall be *standing before the throne and before the Lamb.* Standing before God uncondemned! Heaven really will be heaven for the Christian when he stands before his Maker and Redeemer and enjoys His unhindered presence and fellowship for evermore.

Notice the description of Jesus as *the Lamb.* It is used of Him many times by John in Revelation and it is a very pregnant title. The Lamb speaks to us of sacrifice. We will have cause to look at this in another chapter, but suffice it to say now that believers will only obtain the beatific vision of heaven because Jesus once died on a cross *like that of a lamb without blemish or spot.* (1 Peter 1:19) *Behold the Lamb of God Who takes away the sin of the world.* (John 1:29)- the very sin which bars us from heaven. What joy it will be to see Jesus face to face, the One Who loved us and gave Himself in sacrifice for us. Understandably, we will *follow the Lamb where ever He goes.* (Revelation 14:4) Samuel Rutherford once said 'Heaven and Christ are the same thing. To be in heaven is to be with Christ and to be with Christ is heaven.' Jesus is our heaven and His death the only door. (Notice here that the Lamb is put on the same level as the throne, showing, almost as a sidelight, that Jesus is co-equal with God the Father.)

It will be a consummation of all the conscious and unconscious desires and yearnings of the human heart when *standing before the throne and before the Lamb* we will utter the most exuberant paean of praise to extol the God of all life, light and love. The congregation are depicted as wearing some very special garments. It is to these that we now turn.

3. THE CLOTHES

Those is heaven are *clothed in white robes.* (Revelation 7:9) White speaks to us of purity. Negatively, *nothing unclean shall enter it.* (Revelation 22:27) But which one of us is clean enough in and of himself to stand before God? *The heavens are not clean in His sight; how much less one who is abominable and corrupt, a man who drinks iniquity like water.* (Job 15:15,16) *God is of purer* eyes than to behold evil and canst not look on wrong. (Habakkuk 1:13) *We have all become like one who is unclean, and all our righteous deeds are like a polluted garment.* (Isaiah 64:6) This terrible dilemma and predicament has been supernaturally solved by God Himself. The spotless righteousness which God requires is the spotless righteousness which He provides - freely, to sinners, who, by trusting in Christ, are 'clothed' with the merits and spotlessness of His sinless life, given up in death on the Cross. *He has clothed me with the garments of salvation, He has covered me with the robe of righteousness.* (Isaiah 61:10)

Jesus once told a parable along these lines, the details of which can be found in Matthew 22:1-14. There, the kingdom of heaven is depicted as a great wedding feast. In it, we are all equal; all are sinners, but all are saved sinners, clothed with the wedding garment of Christ's righteousness - *For our sake He made Him to be sin Who knew no sin so that in Him we might become the righteousness of God.* (2 Corinthians 5:21) It is only this which makes us fit for heaven. The parable has a warning though, a warning to those who by-pass Christ's gift of righteousness, maybe by trying to weave their own righteousness on the loom of good works or religious ritual. *When the king came in to look at the guests he saw there a man who had no wedding garment; and he said to him 'Friend, how did you get in here without a wedding garment?' And he was speechless. Then the king said to the attendants, 'Bind him hand and foot, and cast him into outer darkness, there men will weep and gnash their teeth.'* (Matthew 22:11-13) On a happier note though, let us consider the victory of the citizens of heaven:-

4. THE CONQUEST

If the white robes of heaven speak of purity the palm branches speak of victory! Heaven's citizens are *clothed in white robes with palm branches in their hands*. (7:9) Heaven is a victorious place! While our lives here on earth at times seem to go from defeat to defeat, in heaven we will have the final victory and conquest over all that seeks to bring us down - death, disease, demons, depression and despair.

The Christian Faith is a victorious Faith. God has no losers just as the Devil has no winners. The palm branches speak vividly of the Christian's conquest. In chapter 12 of Revelation we see the Devil employing his tactic of accusing Christians, but we also read *they have conquered him by the blood of the Lamb and the word of their testimony*. (12:11) The heavenly palms of victory remind us of Psalm 91:12ff:- *The righteous flourish like the palm tree....They are planted in the house of the Lord, they flourish in the courts of our God... they are ever full of sap and green.*

At the commencement of the week which ended in Jesus' conquest of death by His dying, we read that He rode into Jerusalem on an ass in fulfilment of Zechariah 9:9:- *Lo your king comes to you: triumphant and victorious is He, humble and riding on an ass, on a colt the foal of an ass.* Jesus literally 'stooped to conquer,' riding on to Calvary to give the sinner who trusts in Him the ultimate victory. The crowd on that day may have sensed this as *they took branches of palm trees and went out to meet Him, crying 'Hosanna! Blessed is He Who comes in the Name of the Lord, even the King of Israel.* (John 12:13) He went on to destroy death by dying - and His resurrection on the third day proves that death and

17

the devil are conquered foes - *He disarmed the principalities and powers and made a public example of them, triumphing over them in the Cross.* (Colossians 2:15) The marvel is, that all who believe in Jesus partake and will partake of His victory. The palm branches will be in our hands! *Death is swallowed up in victory. O death, where is thy victory. O death, where is thy sting... Thanks be to God Who gives us the victory through our Lord Jesus Christ.* (1 Corinthians 15:55,57)

Achievements, success and victory in this life is usually achieved - gained by merit. But victory in the Christian sense is solely the gift of God's grace - received by faith in the triumphant Saviour. Said John on a previous occasion:- *this is the victory that overcomes the world, our faith. Who is it that overcomes the world but he who believes Jesus is the Son of God.* (1 John 5:4,5) We need not be surprised therefore at the significant cry which the victorious multinational multitude, clothed in Christ's righteousness are heard to be shouting:-

5. THE CRY

Salvation belongs to our God Who sits upon the throne, and to the Lamb! (Revelation 7:10) is the loud, glad cry of heaven - as indeed it is the fervent and honest confession of every sinner here on earth who has experienced the salvation of Christ, having first been in terror at his lost and helpless state. *Salvation belongs to our God* means that the cause and source of our salvation is God; it is due not to anything in or of ourselves but to God and to Him alone. It is this which distinguishes Christianity from all the religions of the world. In every other religion, men work for their own salvation and by-pass the Cross. Such works are by their nature human and imperfect. Christianity however proclaims a salvation which God Himself has procured and provided for the sinner in the finished Cross-work of Jesus Christ for all who believe. *Deliverance belongs to the Lord.* (Jonah 2:9) *By grace you have been saved through faith, and this is not your own doing, it is the gift of God, not because of works, lest any man should boast.* (Ephesians 2:8,9)

Note carefully that the salvation here is ascribed equally to both *our God... and to the Lamb.* The members of the Trinity of the One God always work in perfect harmony. *God was in Christ reconciling the world to Himself.* (2 Corinthians 5:19) Salvation is due both to the sovereign will of God and the sacrifice of the Lamb. There is no contradiction as God Himself provided the Lamb, even His Own dear Son, for the sinner's salvation (c.f. Genesis 22:8). Salvation is all of God, from the beginning to the end. The glory is therefore all God's - for ever and ever. Which brings us to our final point in this opening chapter. Listen to the words of the chorus of heaven:-

6. THE CHORUS

To know God is to love Him and to see God is to worship Him. It is small wonder then that heaven is characterised by ceaseless worship. *Heaven is my throne* says God in Isaiah 66:1. To worship means 'to ascribe worth' and there is none more worthy than the Almighty God Who sits upon the throne of heaven. 'True worship is based upon recognised greatness, and greatness is superlatively seen in Sovereignty, and at no other footstool will men really worship.'(J.B.Moody)

Here we read of a sevenfold worship of God with two Amens sandwiching them in-between. Seven in the Bible is symbolic of perfection and completeness. Amen means 'it is so,' so two Amens mean it is doubly so! Angels, elders and the four living creatures *fell on their faces and worshipped God, saying 'Amen! Blessing and glory and wisdom and thanksgiving and honour and power and might be to our God for ever and ever! Amen.'* What a climax - but there is more to follow!

To God is ascribed *Blessing. He is the blessed and only Sovereign, the King of kings and Lord of lords.* (1 Timothy 6:15) yet He graciously bestows His blessing on His creatures.

To God is ascribed *glory*, a description which is unique to God, telling of His manifested greatness and 'God-ness.'

To God is ascribed *wisdom. O the depth of the riches and wisdom and knowledge of God,* (Romans 11:33) and in Christ *are hid all the treasures of wisdom and knowledge.* (Colossians 2:3) God is the 'God only wise'- yet in Christ He graciously imparts His wisdom to us for our glorification (c.f. 1 Corinthians 2:7)

To God is ascribed *thanksgiving*. We owe our all to God. How then He deserves our thanks as *from Him and through Him and to Him are all things.* (Romans 11:36)

To God is ascribed *honour*. His alone is the infinite preeminence, and eternal homage belongs to Him by sovereign right.

To God is ascribed *power and might*. God is 'El Shaddai,' the Almighty, All-sufficient One. He is infinite and awesome in His power, as is evidenced by His Creation - which is yet the outskirts of His ways. God's

power and might though is still seen working miracu-
lously, even today, when He saves sinners. Sinners
heading for hell, He turns, and by irresistable grace
makes them His children, raising them from the grave to
glory - to the eternal praise of His glory and grace.

CHAPTER TWO

The Divine Salvation of Heaven

'Who are these, clothed in white robes, and whence have they come?... 'These are they who have come out of the great tribulation, they have washed their robes and made them white in the blood of the Lamb. Therefore are they before the throne of God...'

(Revelation 7:13-15)

It has been aptly said, that whenever we see a 'therefore' in the Bible, we should stop and consider what it is there for. The 'therefore' above relates to the preceding verse. The inhabitants of heaven are *'before the throne of God'* not by chance but because of certain happenings. What happenings? These we will consider now under the title of the Divine Salvation of Heaven. Salvation here, (a general term, concerning God's deliverance; His gracious rescue of His people from peril) is viewed as a consequence of four occurences, namely:- 1. Coming out 2. Cleansing 3. Clothing and 4. Calvary.

1. COMING OUT

These are they who have come out of the great tribulation.

Heaven's salvation here is depicted as a final rest; not a rest in the sense of unconscious sleep, but a welcome rest from all of the trials, tribulations, pains and persecutions of this life here on earth. John the author knew all about tribulation - it was on account of his faith that he was exiled on the Isle of Patmos to begin with, and whilst there he may have been forced to labour in the island's quarries. John's readers also knew all about tribulation, as they were currently being persecuted for their faith most savagely, by the brutal, anti-Christian policies of Emperor Domitian (A.D. 90-95). So what an encouragement it would have been to them to know that those in heaven, their dear friends included, *are they who have come out of the great tribulation* - saved to sorrow and suffer no more.

Salvation as a 'coming out of the great tribulation' would certainly have put iron in the spines of John's first century readers - but this message of hope has also encouraged Christians ever since. Troubles and trials are the lot of the Christian in a fallen world which on the whole rejects Christ and says *We do not want this Man to reign over us.* (Luke 19:14) That is why we read of Paul and Barnabas undertaking their pastoral charge *strengthening the souls of the disciples, exorting them to continue in the Faith saying that through many tribulations we must enter the Kingdom of God.* (Acts 14:22) That was Paul's corporate care, and his individual care was similarly realistic, as we see from his writing to Timothy *Share in suffering as a good soldier of Christ Jesus* (2 Timothy 1:3) .... *all who desire to live a godly life in Christ Jesus will be persecuted.* (2 Timothy 3:12)

Heaven is a land free from tribulation! Jesus said *In the world you have tribulation,* (John 16:38) and no Christian is free from tribulation in this life. As the Puritans used to say, 'we are all subject to losses and crosses.' At times we bring tribulation upon ourselves by our own foolishness; at other times tribulation comes upon us as part of the mystery of Providence - training us to cast ourselves on God more closely. No Christian relishes tribulation, but it is the norm for a Christian who is a Biblical 'non-conformist,' in this world (c.f. Romans 12:2). The Devil hates Christians and *prowls around like a roaring lion seeking someone to devour.* (1 Peter 5:8) We may even suggest that if a Christian is enjoying a totally trial free life in this world, something is amiss, as Jesus taught quite plainly *If the world hates you, know that it has hated Me before it hated you. If you were of the world, the world would love its own; but because you are not of the world, but I chose you out of the world, therefore the world hates you... A servant is not greater than his master. If they persecuted Me they will persecute you.* (John 15:18-20) All these considerations will be blessedly inapplicable in heaven, when we will have fully, finally and forever come out of the great tribulation. Truly, *the sufferings of this present time are not worth comparing with the glory that is to be revealed to us.* (Romans 8:18)

2. CLEANSING

They have washed their robes and made them white in the blood of the Lamb.

In the Bible, sin is considered in terms of a four letter word - dirt. *Nothing unclean shall enter* (heaven). (Revelation 22:27) The problem is, which one of us possesses the requisite purity to stand before a thrice holy God? Not one of us. *Can a man be pure before his Maker?* (Job 4:17)... *the heavens are not clean in His sight; how much less one who is abominable and corrupt, a man who drinks iniquity like water.* (Job

15:15,16) It is when the Holy Spirit convinces us of this fact that we cry out, in unison with David *Wash me thoroughly from my iniquity, and cleanse me from my sin!* (Psalm 51:2)

If the Bible considers sin in terms of dirt and unclean-ness, it also considers salvation in terms of being washed and made clean! *They have washed their robes and made them white in the blood of the Lamb.* This brings us to the very essence of the Christian's salvation, namely that *The blood of Jesus His Son cleanses us from all sin.* (1 John 1:7) Countless Christian hymns have been written on this blessed theme of being washed in the blood of the Lamb, and of the many we quote;-

There is a fountain filled with blood
drawn from Emmanuel's veins
Sinners who plunge beneath that flood
lose all their guilty stains.

In Zechariah 13:1 God promised *On that day there shall be a fountain opened for the house of David and the inhabitants of Jerusalem to cleanse them from sin and unclean-ness,-* and this promise of a Divine washing for the sinner was superabundantly fulfilled in Christ at Calvary, *where one of the soldiers pierced His side with a spear, and at once there came out blood and water.* (John 19:34) Calvary is God's provision of a washing for the unclean sinner, a theme which figures prominantly in the letters of Paul:-

Christ loved the Church and gave Himself up for her, that He might sanctify her having <u>cleansed</u> her by the <u>washing</u> of the water with the Word. (Ephesians 5:26)

Jesus Christ... gave Himself for us... to purify for Himself a people of His Own.. (Titus 3:5)

And after an unholy catalogue of the most modern sounding sins, Paul wrote to the Corinthians *And such were some of you, but you were washed ... in the Name of the Lord Jesus Christ.* (1 Corinthians 6:11)

Salvation thus is a cleansing. *He saved us... by the washing of regeneration and renewal..* (Titus 3:5) This occurs whenever an unclean sinner comes repentantly to Jesus and is washed in His precious blood. 'This blood and nothing else in the universe whitens us so that we may stand before God.'(Lenski) Salvation is a cleansing, but it is also a clothing:-

3. CLOTHING

We have already touched upon this in verse nine. Salvation is viewed as being 'clothed in white robes,' (white signifying purity) and wearing robes made white in the blood of the Lamb. If sin is a defiled state it is also a naked state, with its resultant shame. When Adam sinned (and in him we all sinned, see Romans 5:12) his perverted instinct was to hide from the presence of God in all his guilt and shame. We recall the scene, *the Lord God called to the man, and said to him 'Where are you?' And he said 'I heard the sound of Thee in the garden and I was afraid, because I was naked; and I hid myself.* (Genesis 3:9,10) Sin is thus a naked state, in fear and trembling of God's holy scrutiny. But what was God's answer to sin's naked state? Clothing;- but a clothing at a cost. An innocent animal was taken, killed and *the Lord God made for Adam and for his wife garments of skins and clothed them.* (Genesis 3:21) What a prefigure of

Calvary is this - the only true and lasting covering (atonement) and clothing for the nakedness of sin.

Salvation is being clothed with the spotless garment of Christ's righteousness and thus being rendered fit to stand before God. In John 13 we read of the Jesus the Servant, Who laid aside His garments (4) in service. In John 19, we read of Jesus the Saviour, Who laid aside His garments in sacrifice. *When the soldiers had crucified Jesus, they took His garments and made four parts, one for each soldier; also His tunic. But the tunic was without seam, woven from top to bottom; so they said to one another 'Let us not tear it, but cast lots for it to see whose it shall be.' This was to fulfil the Scripture 'They parted my garments among them, and for my clothing they cast lots.'* (John 19:23,24, c.f. Psalm 22:18)

The death of Jesus was substitutionary. The sinless One gave up His sinless life for sinners, taking the full suffering of the sinner's sin , shame and nakedness, so that whoever believes in Him can rejoice and say *I will greatly rejoice in the Lord, my soul shall exult in my God; for He has clothed me with the garments of salvation, He has covered me with the robe of righteousness.* (Isaiah 61:10)

> *When I stand before the throne*
> *Dressed in beauty not my own*
> *When I see Thee as Thou art*
> *Love Thee with unsinning heart*
> *Then Lord shall I fully know*
> *Not till then how much I owe.*

The Divine salvation of heaven. It is a result of coming out, cleansing and clothing; and to sum up much of what we have considered, it is a result of:-

4. CALVARY

The blood of the Lamb.

This can only refer to Calvary, as it was there that the Lord shed His blood for the sinner's salvation, *for without the shedding of blood there is no forgiveness of sins.* (Hebrews 9:22) John uses the title of 'the Lamb' twenty one times in Revelation for the Lord Jesus, so it is to this that we will now turn and consider briefly:-

When John the Baptist saw Jesus he said *Behold the Lamb of God Who takes away the sin of the world,* (John 1:29) and Peter referred to *the precious blood of Christ, like that of a Lamb without blemish or spot.* (1 Peter 1:19&20) - showing that Calvary was no accident but an appointment; God's Own eternal appointment for the sinner's salvation and His Own eternal glory, even before the world had been created and sin had entered the scene. Hence it was prophesied of Christ that He would be *like a Lamb that is led to the slaughter, and like a sheep that before its shearers is dumb...* (Isaiah 53:7)

The main event which colours the Jewish national consciousness is the Exodus from slavery in Egypt. Here they remember how they escaped from bondage when the Angel of Death passed over their homes but slayed all the first-born in the homes of the Egyptians. The Angel of Death passed over the Israelite's homes however, not automatically but because of the blood of the passover lamb which had been killed. The innocent lamb died to save their first-born from death. Note the details:- *Your lamb shall be without blemish.* (Exodus 12:5) *Take some of the blood and put it on the two doorposts and the lintel of the houses.* (Exodus 12:7)

29

When I see the blood I will pass over you, and no plague shall fall upon you to destroy you. (Exodus 12:13)

All of this prefigured and foreshadowed Christ and His greater Work of redemption. Christ is God's Passover Lamb. His blood, when applied to the human heart saves from the sin which leads to hell - which is the worst plague of all. *Christ our paschal lamb has been sacrificed.* (1 Corinthians 5:7) and as the book of Revelation opens *To Him Who loved us and has freed us from our sins by His blood.* (Revelation 1:5) People, even religious people, may cast scorn and doubt on this, here on earth; but heaven's peal of praise remains *Worthy is the Lamb!* (Revelation 5:12) And from John's privileged position, he recorded for us, *I saw a Lamb standing, as though it had been slain,* (Revelation 5:6) and the heavenly chorus rang out, loud and clear, *Worthy art Thou... for Thou wast slain and by Thy blood didst ransom men for God.* (Revelation 5:9) At this, we who are in the world but not of it, assuming that we have actually been saved by the blood of the Lamb, can only break off and join the heavenly chorus and offer our humble praise to the Lamb once slain:-

Come let us join our cheerful songs with angels round the throne
Ten thousand thousand are their tongues but all their joys are one
"Worthy the Lamb that died" they cry
"to be exalted thus"
"Worthy the Lamb" our lips reply
"For He was slain for us."

CHAPTER THREE

The Divine Shadow of Heaven

Therefore are they before the throne of God.
                              (Revelation 7:15a)

Heaven will be living and dwelling before the throne of the Almighty; thus heaven will be abiding in the shadow of God. The Bible often uses the metaphor of the Divine shadow to describe our safety in God in this life. How precious is *Thy steadfast love, O God! The children of men take refuge in the shadow of Thy wings,* (Psalm 36:7) wrote King David, and how blessedly true this reality is - but in heaven it will be absolutely, literally and eternally so.

In Psalm 17:8 David prayed to his God. Aware of *the wicked who despoil me and of my deadly enemies who surround me,* he prayed *Keep me as the apple of the eye; hide me in the shadow of Thy wings.* Such prayers will be gloriously un-necessary in heaven, when we will live in the absolute security of the shadow of the Almighty forevermore. We sometimes sing;-

So near, so very near to God, nearer I cannot be,
For in the Person of His Son I am as near as He.

and if we are saved we know that it is true; it is true in the positional sense - but in heaven it will be true in the practical sense.

Therefore are they before the throne of God. This will be a place of infinite delights. *With great delight I sat in His <u>shadow</u> and His fruit was sweet to my taste.* (Song of Solomon 2:3) But let us consider the Divine Shadow of Heaven in three ways. It is a place of 1. Nearness 2. Dearness and 3. Clearness.

1. A PLACE OF NEARNESS

But for me it is good to be near God, (Psalm 73:28) wrote the Psalmist. It will indeed be good, as (in the words of the Shorter Catechism) the chief end of man is to glorify God and to enjoy Him forever. Man was made in the image of God, and although this image has been defaced and disfigured by sin, he secretly and unconsciously craves the fellowship with His Maker for which he was designed. As Rene Paschal once reportedly said:- "Every man has a God shaped void in his heart which only God can fill." *Whom have I in heaven but Thee? And there is nothing upon earth that I desire besides Thee.* (Psalm 73:25) Heaven will be the fulfilment of these unconscious desires.

But now, in Christ Jesus you who once were far off have been brought near in the blood of Christ. (Ephesians 2:14) and our intimate nearness to God in heaven will be all the more remarkable when we consider that by nature we are infinitely separated from God by our sins. *Your iniquities have made a separation between you and your God, and your sins have hid His face from you.* (Isaiah 59:2) So heaven's nearness, if attained, is solely the result of God's grace - His undeserved favour and kindness to the undeserving and ill deserving. Heaven's nearness gives us a foothold on understanding the Christian doctrine of reconciliation. Reconciliation refers to the resultant peaceful state and restored relationship between two parties that had previously been opposed. To be reconciled is to be brought together. It is human sin which puts the infinite gulf between God and man. Reconciliation is God's work in which He has taken the initiative in bridging this infinite gap which sin has made - as the following Scriptures show:-

God was in Christ reconciling the world to Himself, not counting their trespasses against them. (2 Corinthians 5:19)

There is one God and there is one mediator between God and men the Man Christ Jesus. (1 Timothy 2:5)

Christ also died for sins once for all, the righteous for the unrighteous that He might bring us to God. (1 Peter 3:18)

Reconciliation and its resultant atonement ('at-one-ment') and nearness to God is thus another of the Calvary blessings wrought by the Lord Jesus Christ. We are reconciled to God now, here on earth, because of His Cross; in heaven we will be reconciled to Him forever - never to leave His blessed shadow. It is then that we will really *rejoice in God through our Lord Jesus Christ through Whom we have now received our reconciliation.* (Romans 5:11) Heaven is a place of nearness. But also, it is:-

2. A PLACE OF DEARNESS

The Divine shadow will be a place of exceeding dearness because we will then be in the immediate presence of God and *God is love.* (1 John 4:8) c.f. Song of Solomon 2:3,4:- *With great delight I sat in His shadow, and His fruit was sweet to my taste. He brought me to the banqueting house, and His banner over me was love.* Who can fathom the love of God in Christ? ...*the love of Christ...surpasses knowledge,* (Ephesians 3:19) wrote Paul.   It is the love of God in Jesus Christ which renders children of wrath children of God, and hell deserving sinners into citizens of the kingdom of heaven. In heaven, a fresh realisation of all this will surely dawn upon us. We will need an eternity to fathom the infinite love of such a God - *that in the coming ages He might show the immeasurable riches of His grace in kindness towards us in Christ Jesus.* (Ephesians 2:7) The Christian owes his salvation solely to the love of the Triune God:-

God the Father: *In this is love not that we loved God but that He loved us and sent His Son to be the propitiation for our sins.* (1 John 4:10)

God the Son: *Christ loved the church and gave Himself up for her.* (Ephesians 5:25)

God the Holy Spirit: *God's love has been poured into our hearts through the Holy Spirit which has been given to us.* (Romans 5:5)

The love of God can only be judged by the infinite cost which He paid for the sinner's salvation, *not with perishable things such as silver or gold but with the precious blood of Christ.* (1 Peter 1:18,19) How dear we must be to the One *Who did not spare His Own Son but gave Him up for us all.* (Romans 8:32). How dear He should be to us when we meditate upon such truths. Alas however, in this life our love for God can fluctuate; not so in heaven though. Abiding in God's shadow we will

realise our dearness to Him afresh and respond in kind.
Love always elicits a response, and in heaven our
response will be unhindered by all earthly limitations
and annoyances:-

When I stand before the throne
Dressed in beauty not my own
When I see Thee as Thou art Love Thee with
unsinning heart
Then Lord shall I fully know Not 'til then how much I
owe.

Heaven: abiding in the shadow of God; a place of
nearness, dearness and thirdly:-

3. A PLACE OF CLEARNESS

In penning his matchless 'hymn to love' in 1 Corinthians
13, Paul included the words *Now we see in a mirror*
dimly, but then face to face. Now I know in part; then I
shall understand fully, even as I have been fully under-
stood. (1 Corinthians 13:12) When we stand before the
throne of God, all the mysteries of this life will fall into
place - or seem entirely irrelevant as we are engulfed in
the sea of His love. This world has much mystery, but in
the Divine shadow, perplexing mystery will give way to
perspicacious clarity.

i. The Vision of God

In heaven *I shall behold Thy face in righteousness.*
(Psalm 17:15) It is a promise on the last page of Scripture
concerning the redeemed in heaven that *they shall see*
His face. (Revelation 22:4) This will involve nearness,

dearness and clearness. It is universally true of all lovers that they have the desire for communion with each other. *Let me see your face, let me hear your voice, for your voice is sweet and your face is comely.* (Song of Solomon 2:14) This is especially so of our relationship with God. Yet how often, alas, is it true that in this fallen world, due to either our own sin or the mystery of Providence, have we been able to relate to the Psalmist when he bemoaned *How long, O Lord? ... How long wilt Thou hide Thy face from me?* (Psalm 13:1) or another Psalmist who prayed *Restore us O Lord of hosts! Let Thy face shine that we may be saved.* (Psalm 80:19)

The highest blessing in the Bible is the blessing of God Himself (c.f. Proverbs 10:22) and this is depicted pertinently in terms of God's face shining upon an individual. The three-fold Aaronic blessing goes:- *The Lord bless you and keep you: the Lord make His face to shine upon you and be gracious to you. The Lord lift up His countenance upon you and give you peace.* (Numbers 6:24-26) and this seeped into the Psalms of Israel written years later:- *May God be gracious to us and bless us and make His face to shine upon us.* (Psalm 67:1) These prayers will be blessedly answered in heaven. There we will see Him face to face and behold His glory, just as Jesus desired (see John 17:24). How clear will our vision then be, undimmed by the shortsightedness of sin. Then we will indeed *Look to Him and be radiant so (your) faces shall never be ashamed.* (Psalm 34:5)

ii. The Veracity of God

Godly old Job, after His great vision of God, was led to confess *I know that Thou canst do all things, and that no purpose of Thine can be thwarted.* (Job 42:2) It is only from heaven's vantage point that we will know truly that this is so and that truly, *in everything God works for good with those who love Him.* (Romans 8:28) This world has many mysteries, not least of which is the problem of suffering. Why do bad things happen to God's people? The problem is as old as the book of Job - itself the oldest book in the world. God is under no obligation to explain His ways to us. Whilst it is true that *Thy Word is a light to my feet and a lamp to my path* (Psalm 119:105) it is also true that *The secret things belong to the Lord our God,* (Deuteronomy 29:29) and *My thoughts are not your thoughts, neither are your ways My ways, says the Lord. For as the heavens are higher than the earth, so are My ways higher than your ways and My thoughts than your thoughts.* (Isaiah 55:8,9) Hence in the meantime, of necessity *we walk by faith, not by sight,* (2 Corinthians 5:7) living by God's promises rather than by explanations.

In heaven, faith will be turned gloriously into sight! We will know then that even the dark, dire and desperate circumstances of our lives were all ordained by God for our good. How we will then exclaim *Ascribe greatness to our God!... His work is perfect; for all His ways are justice.* (Deuteronomy 32:3,4) It is this which Anne R. Cousins put into verse so well. When, picturing herself in the land of glory and looking back over life's trials, she penned:-

> *With mercy and with judgement*
> *My web of time He wove*
> *And aye the dews of sorrow*
> *Were lustered by His love*

I' ll bless the hand that guided
I' ll bless the heart that planned
When throned where glory dwelleth
In Immanuel' s land.

Immanuel's land! It will be living in the Divine shadow
- a place of unsurpassed nearness, dearness and clearness.

CHAPTER FOUR

The Divine Service of Heaven

They.... serve Him day and night within His temple...
(Revelation 7:15b)

PERFECT EMPLOYMENT :
PERFECT ENJOYMENT

It comes as a surprise to some when they realise that, according to the Bible, there is work to be done in heaven! This requires some definition and explanation, lest it seem to contradict the equal emphasis that the Bible teaches concerning heaven as being a state of 'rest.' *'Blessed are the dead who die in the Lord henceforth.' 'Blessed indeed,' says the Spirit,' that they may rest from their labours, for their deeds follow them!'* (Revelation 14:13) *For we who have believed enter that rest.* (Hebrews 4:3) *So then, there remains a sabbath rest for the people of God; for whoever enters God's rest also ceases from his labours as God did from His.* (Hebrews 4:9,10) These verses suggest that heaven is an eternal Sabbath rest, that is, completely devoted to God having completed our earthly work and responsibilities and now receiving the eternal good of the finished Work of Christ.

The 'rest' of heaven would have been good and wel-come news to John's first readers, persecuted for their faith as they were, along with its consequent hardship and even martyrdom. How they would have relished knowing that their loved ones in heaven *were each given a white robe and told to rest a little longer*. (Revelation 6:11)

The 'rest' of heaven is a blessed reality. However, the Bible also teaches that in heaven we will *serve Him day and night within His temple*. Yes. Heaven will be a rest from all the labours, trials and struggles with the sin within and without, which is so much part and parcel of this life on earth; but far from being a 'holy inactivity,' in heaven we will have plenty to do! In heaven we will realise our chief end and take infinite delight in serving our Maker constantly and continually, free from all of the weakness, staleness and weariness which character-ises our work here on earth. Our work in heaven will be our worship! *And His servants shall worship Him,* (Revelation 22:3) and there is no higher activity in which we can engage than ascribing worth directly to our God.

EARTHLY EMPLOYMENT: THE OBLIGATION

Work is as equally a Divine ordinance as marriage or the Sabbath. *Six days shall you labour and do all your work*. (Exodus 20:8) Even before the Fall, we read that *The Lord God took the man and put him in the garden of Eden to till it and keep it*. (Genesis 2:15) Thus it comes as nothing unusual to see that work will be part of the heavenly life too, as heaven is paradise restored. The Apostle Paul often included the field of work in his Apostolic exhortations - and as a Pharisee, he would have had less of the modern distinction between the sacred and the secular; all was to be done to the glory of God.(Luther, at the time of the Reformation also emphasised the Christian's vocation, and purported that a Christian cobbler had no less a calling than a Christian preacher, the difference being only one of role and function.) And so Paul exhorted *Slaves, obey in everything those who are your earthly masters, not with eyeservice, as men pleasers, but in singleness of heart, fearing the Lord. Whatever your task, work heartily, as serving the Lord and not men...* (Colossians 3:22,23)

It follows therefore, that if work is a normal part of life, it will also be a normal part of eternal life; the life in heaven has notable similarities to, as well as notable differences from, our life on earth. Paul certainly saw work as integral to the redeemed life. He would have agreed with William Booth, the founder of the Salvation Army, that we are 'saved to serve.' Our creed is expressed in deed - faith works! Thus *Let the thief no longer steal, but rather let him labour with his hands, so that he may be able to give to those in need.* (Ephesians 4:28) And after extolling the saving grace of God apart from any human works, Paul nevertheless continued *For we are His workmanship, created in Christ Jesus for good works, which God prepared beforehand that we should walk in them.* (Ephesians 2:10)

EARTHLY UNEMPLOYMENT: THE CONSTERNATION

Unemployment is one of the social plagues of the late twentieth century. At the time of writing, the unemployment figures here in the United Kingdom almost reach the three million mark. Figures are difficult to interpret. The figures could be higher or lower. Some people do not want work as they find it financially more worthwhile to claim benefit than to take a low paid job. Other people are 'moonlighting,' that is they are officially unemployed but also earning money by jobs 'on the side.' Whilst other people are genuinely unemployed; they crave to be in work yet, due to a variety of factors,(such as redundancy, the recession, high technology, the increase in women now going out to work,) they find themselves out of work and having to go through the indignity of 'signing on.'

The heartache of being genuinely unemployed can only be truly felt if one has actually experienced it first hand. A stock conversation opener goes 'What do you do then?' - to which the response is an embarrassed shuffling of the shoes, looking to the floor and muttering. Unemployment has a social stigma. The feeling that one is a 'sponger' is deeply ingrained. Then there is also the financial hardship. When one has a growing family to maintain this is difficult to bear. Cuts have to be made. 'You can't have it' becomes a motto. Unemployment blurs the edges between work and leisure. Leisure becomes work. Nothing seems special about the weekend when one is home all week. Unemployment also puts a heavy strain on a marriage. Traditionally, women would stay at home and be the home-maker, whilst men would go out to work to keep the family. Having a man about the house all day increases marital stress and 'in-fighting.' Then there is the overall demoralising effect of unemployment. Having no work can make one feel useless and worthless. We are often defined by what we do rather than who we are. Long term unemployment causes a gradual lowering of self-esteem. Having boxes and boxes of job rejection slips (due to maybe three hundred applicants for just one post) eventually wears down the morale of the strongest. How good then that in heaven there is work for all! No more 'dole' then. Gladly *they shall serve Him day and night within His temple.*

EARTHLY EMPLOYMENT: THE VEXATION

Actual employment here on earth however is not always the proverbial 'bed of roses.' We live in a fallen world. Sin and its consequences has infected every department of life, and one of its consequences is told plainly in Scripture:- *cursed is the ground because of you; in toil you shall eat of it all the days of your life; thorns and thistles it shall bring forth to you; and you shall eat the plants of the field. In the sweat of your face you shall eat bread.* (Genesis 3:17-19) Work on earth involves toil and fatigue.

There is nothing better for a man than he should....find enjoyment in his toil. (Ecclesiastes 2:24) But just who does find real enjoyment and fulfilment in his work? Those who do are the favoured few, as much work is repetitive, unfulfilling, uncreative, tedious and irksome. Work can entail standing at an endless production line, digging coal underground in a dark cramped space, being 'chained to a desk' or looking at an impersonal computer screen for most of the day. It is small wonder then that people seek to find their enjoyment and fulfilment in their leisure time. How long the hours of work can seem. How eager we can be to clock off and start 'living'- a creative hobby, an exciting sport, being part of a team where we feel valued (or on a baser level, living out ones' fantasies via a movie screen or even seeking to escape through drugs or alchohol.)

When work is scarce, compromises have to be made as regards ones' ideal job. How good it would be if we could channel our gifts and talents into our work - but few people have the opportunity so to do. Thus it is in their leisure time that people seek 'escapism,' and, for example, join an amateur dramatic society, play a musical instrument, join a choir, teach a skill to a handicapped person. Unemployment is awful, but employment is often something to endure rather than to enjoy, notwithstanding.

HEAVENLY EMPLOYMENT:
THE TRANSFORMATION

We can take great heart from the prospect that in heaven, our employment will be more exciting and fulfilling *than all that we ask or think*. (Ephesians 3:20) Heaven will be marked by perfect employment bringing perfect enjoyment to the participant, surpassing the highest that earth can offer. Whilst we had better not say much more on the subject, lest we end up speculating beyond what Scripture has revealed, we may be sure that heaven's work will be like the most ideal work for us on earth which we can imagine, tailor made for our physical and psychological frame, multiplied by infinity! We may get some hints on this from Revelation 21:24,26 where we read of heaven that *the kings of the earth shall bring their glory into it... they shall bring into it the glory and honour of the nations*. We may interpret this to mean that all that is truly good and beautiful in this world will not be lost in the next, but infinitely enhanced, and each individual and nation will make a distinctive contribution to heaven's work and service, to the glory of God and their own eternal joy and well-being.

PERFECT EMPLOYMENT:
PERFECT ENJOYMENT

To summarise much of what we have said, there is work in heaven. It is a land of perfect employment and perfect enjoyment as there, *They... serve Him day and night within His temple*. Such work will be a glorious undertaking and will know nothing of the failure, frustration and fatigue of its counterpart here on earth. Let us let a theologian from a former generation have the final say on this matter;-

' The motive which actuates the saints on earth is the same in principle, though not so intense, as that which actuates the saints in glory, whose constant delight is to perform the noblest actions and service, namely that of praising God and punctually performing His will without interruptions or defeats. As they have always a ravishing sense of His goodness to them, so they exercise their perfectly pure minds in ascriptions of praise and glory to Him for delivering them from deserved ruin, and placing them in the blissful mansions where they find themselves possessed of ease, delight, complacency and glory wholly unmerited.' (Boettner.)

CHAPTER FIVE

The Divine Shelter of Heaven

He Who sits upon the throne will shelter them with His presence. (Revelation 7:15)

or as an alternative translation has it:-

He Who sits on the throne will spread His tent over them. (N.I.V.)

However we translate the above verse, we can be certain that in heaven we will enjoy both

1. THE SOVEREIGN PROTECTION OF GOD, and
2. THE SOVEREIGN PRESENCE OF GOD.

In heaven, God will shelter His people from all harm by the glory (the ancient 'Shekinah') of His abiding presence. (The description 'Sovereign' is employed above as our text describes God as being *upon the throne.* This is so throughout Revelation, not to mention the whole Bible. God is the *God Who is seated on the throne.* (Revelation 19:4) This would have been a great comfort to John's readers, considering the tumultuous times in which they were living - as it has been a great comfort for believers ever since. The total and absolute sovereignty of God is one of the truly majestic themes of the Bible. *Hallelujah! For the Lord our God the Almighty reigns.* (Revelation 19:6)

1. THE SOVEREIGN PROTECTION OF GOD

He Who sits upon the throne will shelter them.

i. The Devil's Schemes

Life on earth is loaded with dangers. The Devil, although possessing limited powers, as he is not omnipotent, is still very much on active service here on earth. God's people here are not immune from harm, and may go through all kinds of physical, social, psychological and even spiritual suffering before they reach glory.

These words are being written from the City of Belfast in Northern Ireland, United Kingdom. It is true to say of here that *I see violence and strife in the city.* (Psalm 55:9) Terrorism abounds in Northern Ireland. It can be a tense and very fearful place in which to live. It is the land of the bomb and the bullet, with a strong military and paramilitary presence.

Evil and danger are a fact of life in this fallen world, so Jesus taught us to pray *Deliver us from evil.* (Matthew 6:13) Evil has a very ancient pedigree. It was equally as real and contentious to Paul in the first century as it is to the citizens of Belfast in the late twentieth. Thus Paul wrote encouragingly to the Thessalonians reminding them *the Lord is faithful, He will strenghthen you and guard you from evil.* (2 Thessalonians 3:3) Evil first appeared on our scene in the Garden of Eden, in the person of the Serpent, *that ancient serpent, who is the Devil and Satan,* (Revelation 20:2) whose origins are shrouded in mystery, despite the hints which we have in

Isaiah 14 and Ezekiel 28.

ii. The Divine Shelter

Throughout the Bible, God is revealed as the sovereign protector of His people and their only dependable source of security. David certainly knew his fair share of danger as he was relentlessly pursued by King Saul and his army. It was from such experiences that he composed Psalms such as *Deliver me from my enemies, O my God, protect me from those who rise up against me, deliver me from those who work evil, and save me from blood thirsty men.* (Psalm 59:1,2) David found his security in his God, for *in Thee my soul takes refuge; in the shadow of Thy wings I will take refuge, till the storms of destruction pass by.* (Psalm 57:1)

We get a vivid example of God's protection in Exodus 14, as the people of Israel were being pursued by the army of Egypt. Humanly speaking, the army of Pharaoh should have slaughtered Israel. How could Israel, including her women and children, have any chance against Pharaoh's chariots and army which included *six hundred picked chariots and all the other chariots of Egypt with officers over them* (Exodus 14:7) when they were untrained for warfare? The answer may be found in Exodus 14:19,20. God provided a wall of protection for His people. He indeed 'sheltered them with His presence.' ...*the Angel of God who went before the host of Israel moved and went behind them; and the pillar of cloud moved from before them and stood behind them, coming between the host of Egypt and the host of Israel. And there was the cloud and the darkness, and the night passed without one coming near the other all night.*

Perhaps the classic expression of God's protection is Psalm 91. This being so we quote it extensively:-

He who dwells in the shelter of the Most High, who abides in the shadow of the Almighty, will say to the Lord, 'My refuge and my fortress; my God in Whom I trust.' For He will deliver you from the snare of the fowler and from the deadly pestilence; He will cover you with His pinions, and under His wings you will find refuge; His faithfulness is a shield and buckler. You will not fear the terror of the night nor the arrow that flies by day, nor the pestilence that stalks in darkness, nor the destruction that wastes at noonday.....

Because you have made the Lord your refuge, the Most High your habitation, no evil shall befall you, no scourge come near your tent....

Because he cleaves to Me in love, I will deliver him; I will protect him because he know My Name....

In considering the security of the believer in God, we face a puzzle. Just what sort of security has the believer in this life? It is certainly not a complete insulation from all evil and harm - Scripture and experience teach us otherwise. Is it not then more of an inner security, the security of faith in a faithful God which remains constant whatever the external trials? Jesus once prayed for His followers, *I do not pray that Thou shouldst take them out of the world, but that Thou shouldst keep them from the evil one.* (John 17:15) Jesus also said to His disciples *Peace I leave with you; My peace I give to you; not as the world gives do I give to you. Let not your hearts be troubled, neither let them be afraid.* (John 14:27)

It is only in heaven that we will have absolute security - fully, finally and forever, when God *will shelter them with His presence.* Even the protection of God however

50

will not be as blessed as the God Who provides the protection! Being sheltered by God will be indescribably sweet, *His banner over me was love.* (Song of Solomon 2:4) And so we move onto:-

2. THE SOVEREIGN PRESENCE OF GOD

He who sits upon the throne will shelter them with His presence, reads our verse. The New Bible Commentary suggests:-

'Charles translates the last part of the verse, 'He that sitteth upon the throne shall cause His Shekinah to abide upon them.' The phrase is unique. The Shekinah was the manifestation of God's presence amongst men, especially in the Tabernacle and the Temple at Jerusalem. After the pilgrimage through the wilderness it was of very rare occurence in Israel; to the Christian it has proved a constant privilege.'

Heaven may be defined as being in the immediate presence of God and enjoying unhindered fellowship with Him, thus fulfilling the ultimate purpose and destiny of man. *Behold, the dwelling of God is with men. He will dwell with them, and they shall be His people, and God Himself will be with them.* (Revelation 21:3)

The outstanding earthly reality that the Bible teaches is that God takes up residence with His people. The blessed heavenly reality of the Bible is that people take up residence with their God. Experientially, the latter is the same as the former except gloriously magnified in its intensity.

More happy but not more secure,
the glorified saints in heaven.

51

Let us ponder then:-

A. GOD'S TERRESTRIAL PRESENCE WITH HIS PEOPLE

and

B. GOD'S CELESTIAL PRESENCE WITH HIS PEOPLE.

A. GOD'S TERRESTRIAL PRESENCE WITH HIS PEOPLE

But will God indeed dwell on earth? Behold, heaven and the highest heaven cannot contain Thee. (1 Kings 8:27) asked Solomon. Staggeringly, the answer is in the affirmative. The God Whose glory fills the heavens stoops down and in an act of gracious condescension, dwells with His people on earth. Let us see Him :-

i. In the Sanctuary

Almost the whole of Exodus 25-40 is devoted to the details of the Tabernacle; its construction, furnishing and purpose. The Tabernacle was a large portable tent, and was the focal point of Israel's religious life at that time. Although the Tabernacle was very elaborate in its Divine instructions, its intent was clear:- *Let them make Me a sanctuary, that I may dwell in their midst.* (Exodus 25:8) And the result *when Moses finished the work (Exodus 40:33)* was this: *the cloud covered the tent of meeting, and the glory of the Lord filled the tabernacle. And Moses was not able to enter the tent of meeting because the cloud abode upon it, and the glory of the*

Lord filled the tabernacle. (Exodus 40:34,35)

In the time of King Solomon, the portable tabernacle became the permanent temple. It was equally, if not more elaborate in its construction, although having the same basic blueprint as the tabernacle. Again, when all of the building work was completed:- *when the priests came out of the holy place, a cloud filled the house of the Lord, so that the priests could not stand to minister because of the cloud; for the glory of the Lord filled the house of the Lord.* (1 Kings 8:10,11)

This glorious presence was not permanent however. Ezekiel informs us how *the glory of the Lord went up from the midst of the city.* (Ezekiel 11:23) The glory of the Lord was forfeited by Israel because of their disobedience and idolatry. But all was not lost. Ezekiel looked forward to better days, and among God's future promises through His prophet, we read of the following:- *My dwelling place shall be with them; and I will be their God, and they shall be My people... when My sanctuary is in the midst of them forevermore.* (Ezekiel 37:27,28) Yes, God manifested His glorious presence in the ancient sanctuaries of Israel. But even more remarkably, God manifested His presence:-

ii. In the Saviour

In the Lord Jesus Christ we see more than a partial fulfilment of Ezekiel's prophecy. It was written of His incarnation that *the Word became flesh and dwelt* (or 'was tabernacled') *among us, full of grace and truth, we have beheld His glory* (c.f. the Shekinah), *glory as of the only Son from the Father.*(John 1:14)

Jesus Christ was the physical presence of God amongst men. He is *'Emmanuel' which means, 'God with us.'*

(Matthew 1:23) He is God become Man. On the whole, His glory was veiled as He walked this soil, yet at the time of the transfiguration something of His Divine splendour broke through. *He reflects the glory of God and bears the very stamp of His nature.* (Hebrews 1:3)- but when He comes the Second time, all will *see the Son of Man coming on the clouds of heaven with power and great glory.* (Matthew 24:30)

iii. In the Sinner

If the incarnation of Christ was an act of humility, what of today? Today God dwells within sinners! By His Holy Spirit, Almighty God presences Himself among men and actually lives in earthen, human vessels. Jesus said:- *If a man loves Me, He will keep My Word, and My Father will love him, and we will come to him and make Our home with him.* (John 14:23)

Do you not know that your body is a temple of the Holy Spirit within you which you have from God.(1 Corinthians 6:19) - an outstanding affirmation when we consider the kind of people the Corinthians used to be (see 6:9-11), and equally outstanding if we know anything about our own hearts.

So we see that God makes His presence with His people here on earth, but one day, God will make His presence with His people more abundantly in heaven. To this we now turn.

B. GOD'S CELESTIAL PRESENCE WITH HIS PEOPLE

In heaven, returning to our text *He Who sits upon the throne will shelter them with His presence,* (or 'cause

His Shekinah glory to abide upon them.') This will be the heaven of heavens! Christians can know a degree of heaven on earth, but this is just a foretaste of the greater reality to come - enjoying the very presence of God Himself in glory.

Jesus once prayed *Father, I desire that they also, whom Thou hast given Me, may be with Me where I am, to behold My glory which Thou hast given Me in Thy love for Me before the foundation of the world.* (John 17:24) He then went on to Calvary and shed His precious blood for sinners, thus making possible an answer to His prayer. In heaven, Jesus' prayer will be fully answered, when the redeemed finally *obtain the glory of our Lord Jesus Christ,* (2 Thessalonians 2:14) and enjoy the shelter of God's presence for all eternity. If God has made His home with us here on earth, we can be sure that one day, we will make our home with Him in heaven!

O sweet and blessed country, the home of God's elect
O sweet and blessed country, that eager hearts expect
Jesus, in mercy bring us, to that dear land of rest,
Who art with God the Father, and Spirit ever blest.

CHAPTER SIX

The Divine Satisfaction of Heaven

They shall hunger no more, neither thirst any more;(Revelation 7: 16a)

THE ABSENCE OF LOSS

So far, we have been considering heaven in terms of its blessed 'positives and presents.' Verse 16 of Revelation 7 however sheds light on heaven it terms of its blessed 'negatives and absences,' that is to say, being free from the many typical ills, trials and torments which beset the people of God here on earth. John seems to be echoing Isaiah 49:10 in his description:- *they shall not hunger or thirst, neither scorching wind nor sun shall smite them, for He Who has pity on them will lead them, and by springs of water will guide them.*

Let us now consider the first line of verse 16. *They shall hunger no more, neither thirst any more.* Whilst the verse is primarily negative, referring to the absence of want, by implication it is strongly postive, suggesting that in heaven we will not only have no unsatisfied desires, but also we shall be totally and positively, fully satisfied. Heaven is a place of Divine satisfaction. In heaven, the redeemed will never have the sense of 'is this all?' or 'there must be more than this' or 'something's missing' which is our frequent experience on earth. In heaven, all of our needs and desires will be fully met, and that satisfaction is pre-eminantly found in the Lamb of God, God's Own provision. *God will provide Himself the Lamb* (Genesis 22:8) and in heaven the redeemed will enjoy God's all sufficient portion for all eternity.

THE ABUNDANT LIFE

Throughout the Bible, the redeemed life is viewed in terms of abundance rather than abstinence, a feast as opposed to a fast. Paul closed his happy letter to the Philippians on an assuring tone by saying *My God will supply every need of yours according to His riches in glory in Christ Jesus.* (Philippians 4:19)

Jesus once made an affirmation *I came that they may have life and have it abundantly.* (John 10:10) Interestingly, the only miracle Jesus performed which is related by all four of the Gospel writers, is the 'Feeding of the 5,000,' (which in actual fact was more like a 'Feeding of the 10,000, as women and children were not included in the count.) The fourfold witness to this miracle - see Matthew 14:13-21; Mark 6:30-44; Luke 9:11-17 and John 6:5-13 - would suggest that the Holy Spirit is concerned that we know the truth concerning the generosity of the God Who is *abounding in steadfast love.* (Psalm 145:8) *Thou openest Thy hand, Thou satisfiest the desire of every living thing.* (Psalm 145:16)

What a picture the 'Feeding of the 5,000' gives us of the Christian life! *They all ate and were satisfied. And they took up twelve baskets full of the broken pieces left over.* (Matthew 14:20) The Christian life is feasting with

Christ! It is enjoying and being totally satisfied with the ample and abundant provision which He has made. *Thou preparest a table for me in the presence of my enemies.* (Psalm 23:5) *What shall I render to the Lord for all His bounty to me?* (Psalm 116:12) *He brought me to the banqueting house and His banner over me was love.* (Song of Solomon:2:4)

THE ABOUNDING LORD

In Exodus 16, we see the wonderful ways of the wonderful God Who provides for His peoples' needs. Jesus taught us to pray *Give us each day our daily bread,* (Luke 11:3) and in Exodus 16 we see the Lord providing daily bread for His people - manna from heaven in the barren wilderness. *Behold, I will rain bread from heaven for you; and the people shall go out and gather a day's portion every day.* (Exodus 16:4) .....*Now the house of Israel called its name 'manna.'* (Exodus 16:31) This was the people of Israel's all-sufficient portion to sustain them as they journeyed through the wilderness. *He that gathered much had nothing over, and he that gathered little had no lack.* (Exodus 16:35) *And the people of Israel ate the manna forty years, till they came to the borders of the land of Canaan,* (Exodus 16:35) as when they eventually left the barren wilderness and entered into Canaan, 'the land flowing with milk and honey,' we read that *the manna ceased on the morrow, when they ate of the produce of the land; and the people of Israel had manna no more, but ate of the fruit of the land of Canaan that year.* (Joshua 5:12)

This 'bread from heaven' which satisfied the physical need of the Israelites was a type of the Lord Jesus Christ.

He is the real 'Bread from Heaven' who meets the spiritual need of all *those who hunger and thirst for righteousness.* (Matthew 5:6) In saying this we speak with Christ's Own authority, for He stated *I am the living bread which came down from heaven; if any one eats of this bread he will live forever; and the bread which I shall give for the life of the world is My flesh.* (John 6:51

> *Jesus of Thee we ne' er will tire*
> *The new and living food*
> *can satisfy our heart's desire*
> *And life is in Thy blood.*

THE ANCIENT LAW

Festivals and Feasts figure quite prominantly throughout the whole of the Bible. In Old Testament times, the Lord instituted seven feasts for His people to observe, benefit from and enjoy. We can read about these in Leviticus 23, in which the regulations for observing the various feast's are given. The feasts commanded there are the feasts of the:- Passover, Unleavened Bread, Firstfruits, Weeks, Trumpets, Atonement and Booths, and all could be considered as solemn, community celebrations. (Later, the feast of Purim was added - see the book of Esther.) With New Testament eyes we see that the feasts speak loudly and multifariously of Christ, even down to their small details.

Believers today observe a simple feast, the Lord's Supper, in obedience to the One Who broke bread and poured out a cup of wine commanding *Do this in remembrance of Me.* (1 Corinthians 11:24) Believers do this, looking back to Calvary in remembrance of His body broken and His blood shed on the Cross for the sinner's salvation.

It is also true to say that the Word of God is a 'feast' for the believer. It is God's Word which encourages us and sustains us as we make our way through this earthly wilderness. *Thy words were found, and I ate them, and Thy words became to me a joy and the delight of my heart.* (Jeremiah 15:16) *How sweet are Thy words to my taste, sweeter than honey to my mouth.* (Psalm 119:103)

THE AFFLUENT LAND

Returning to our opening text, having considered what we have about the Divine generosity, it comes as less of a surprise that heaven will be a place of total satisfaction. *They shall hunger no more neither thirst any more.* The heavenly feast will be a Feast to end all feasts. Any earthly joy is just a foretaste of these greater things to come, (c.f. 2 Corinthians 5:5, when the phrase *Spirit as a guarantee* of the greater heavenly life, could be paraphrased 'a foretaste of better things to come.') Revelation terms the Feast of Heaven as the 'Marriage Supper of the Lamb.' *Blessed are those who are invited to the marriage supper of the Lamb.* (Revelation 19:9)

The idea of the Kingdom of Heaven as being, amongst other things, a feast, is not unique to the book of Revelation, but can be traced back to Him of Whom Revelation speaks. Jesus, the Lamb of Revelation, during the last few days before the time He was actually slain, taught a certain parable. This began *The kingdom of heaven may be compared to a king who gave a marriage feast for his son, and sent his servants to call those who were invited to the marriage feast..* (Matthew

22:1-3, c.f. Luke 14:15-24) However, glimpses of heaven as being a satisfying feast predate even the words of Jesus. In Isaiah 25, a chapter which is distinctly eschatalogical - *He will swallow up death for ever* (Isaiah 25:8) - Isaiah gives us a clear view of the future heavenly feast, remarkable considering the time in which he lived. *On this mountain the Lord of hosts will make for all peoples a feast of fat things, a feast of wine on the lees, of fat things full of marrow, of wine on the lees well refined.* (Isaiah 25:6)

So we see that the Bible is one. It has One ultimate author, and only one way of salvation from the miry slime (Psalm 40:2) to the Marriage Supper.

THE AMAZING LOVE

In closing, we may say that the Feast of God is the provision of God - the abundant provision which God has made in Christ for the salvation and satisfaction of perishing sinners. Jesus said *My flesh is food indeed and My blood is drink indeed.* (John 6:55) (Here He was not referring to the communion as that was not instituted until John 13.)

God Himself knows our need of salvation, and in the giving of His Son on the Cross He has superabundantly provided for our need a feast which will both save us from perishing and satisfy us eternally. Paradoxically, Jesus Christ is both the host and the feast! In heaven it will be true to say *when I awake I shall be satisfied with beholding Thy form.* (Psalm 17:15) *as in Thy presence there is fullness of joy, in Thy right hand are pleasures forevermore.* (Psalm 16:11)

In heaven they shall hunger no more, neither thirst any more. Why? Because of Jesus Who promised *I am the bread of life. He who comes to Me shall not hunger and he who believes in Me shall never thirst.* (John 6:35)

Heaven is thus is a place of Divine satisfaction. There, we shall be completely satisfied with Christ as our portion - but even more amazingly, He shall be satisfied with us as His portion! When we are in glory, enjoying our satisfaction in Christ, it is then that *He shall see the fruit of the travail of His soul and be satisfied.* (Isaiah 53:11)

> *What food luxurious loads the board*
> *When at His table sits the Lord*
> *The wine how rich, the bread how sweet*
> *When Jesus deigns His guests to meet.*

CHAPTER SEVEN

The Divine Security of Heaven

the sun shall not strike them, nor any scorching heat.
(Revelation 7:16)

THE PARADOX OF GOOD

It is a strange fact of this life, that even good and useful things can cause us harm. Water is essential for life - but the same water which quenches our thirst and cleanses our bodies can also cause us to drown. Gas and electricity are great conveniences, providing light and heat for our homes - yet the same substances, if not kept in check, are capable of causing great damage, destruction and even death. Examples of this fine dividing line between a blessing and a bane could be multiplied, and the example pertinent to our text for this chapter is that of the sun.

THE PARADISE OF GLORY

Nothing could be more pleasant than basking in the sun on summer holiday - yet too much of this good thing can cause unpleasant sunburn and in the long term, even skin cancer. No such harm or hurt will ever come upon the inhabitants of heaven however, as it is a place of infinite safety and security where *the sun shall not strike them, nor any scorching heat.* What a contrast this is to those who are under the wrath of God:-

THE PERDITION OF GEHENNA

As an eternal Paradise awaits the believer in Jesus, likewise, most formidably, an eternal peril awaits those who have refused God's offer of mercy. The book of Revelation is as equally candid in describing the plight of such, in terms diametrically opposed to our opening verse:- *The fourth angel poured out his bowl on the sun, and it was allowed to scorch men with fire; men were scorched by the fierce heat, and they cursed the name of God.* (Revelation 16:8,9)

THE PROTECTION OF GOD

As we saw in a previous chaper, the Bible teaches us very clearly that God is the Sovereign Protector of His people. With so many of the harsher elements surrounding them, threatening their welfare, God's people are yet safe under His Fatherly shield.

The land of Israel is a much warmer land than where these words are being written, here in the temperate climate of Northern Ireland. A visit to Israel once by the present writer especially brought to life a verse of the Bible which echoes the thought of the verse we are considering. Sitting in the shade amongst a fierce, dry middle-eastern heat, it is much easier to understand *The Lord is your keeper; the Lord is your shade on your right hand. The sun shall not smite you by day, nor the moon by night.* (Psalm 121:5,6)

Still with this Divine security in mind, Isaiah the prophet likewise shows us that what is true of the heaven of God is also true of the God of heaven.(As an aside, we often say that a home tells us something about its inhabitant - it is interesting to observe how different college students decorate and customise their rooms.) Heaven is the place of God's safe-keeping! There, we will be forever safe, secure and shielded from the harsher elements of this world which seek to hurt and harm us. Let us let Isaiah speak. He says of the God of heaven, *Thou hast been a stronghold to the poor, a stronghold to the needy in his distress, a shelter from the storm and a shade from the heat; for the blast of the ruthless is like a storm against a wall, like heat in a dry place.* (Isaiah 25:4,5) And on the same note, earlier on in his prophecy, Isaiah gives us a passage which seems to look above and beyond any earthly Jerusalem into the New Jerusalem of heaven itself. It's description is in line with everything we have glimpsed so far:- *Then the Lord will create over the whole rite of Mount Zion and over her assemblies a cloud by day, and smoke and the shining of a flaming fire by night; for over all the glory there will be a canopy and a pavilion. It will be a shade by day from the heat, and for a refuge and a shelter from the storm and rain.* (Isaiah 4:5,6) Truly, at that time, we will say as never before *Thou, O Lord, art a shield about me, my glory and the lifter of my head.* (Psalm 3:3)

THE PERIL OF GODLESSNESS

The Bible teaches us by contrast as well as by straight teaching. No where is this more so than in what it reveals concerning hell. Hell is the complete opposite of heaven, and nowhere is this antithesis brought out more clearly than against the background of what we are considering now. If in heaven *the sun shall not strike them nor any scorching heat,* hell is the place of *everlasting burnings,* (c.f. Isaiah 33:14) and the place of *the punishment of eternal fire.* (Jude 7) It is indescribably awful - as the reality will be worse than any language can capture. Yet the Bible, the Book which tells us how we can be saved from this eternal damnation, by way of warning us, pulls no punches in its description of the plight of those who reject God's offer of salvation. *This is the second death, the lake of fire; and if any one's name was not found written in the book of life, he was thrown into the lake of fire.* (Revelation 20:14,15) What a contrast to the safety, security and serenity implied in the verse with which we began this chapter.

Lest we are in any doubt about hell's severity, even the Lord Jesus, the lovliest, tenderest Man Who ever graced this earth, once told a parable in which a man went to hell. There he cried out in an agonising howl, *I am in anguish in this flame.* (Luke 16:24) Jesus certainly believed in hell. If there was no hell, would the Cross have been so necessary? 'The Scripture tells us that in hell are three things: there is darkness, there is fire and there are chains. Hell is an abiding place but no resting place.'(Thomas Watson.)

THE PROPITIATION OF GOLGOTHA

The believer need not fear the fires of hell.Those fires, frightening though they are, will be identical in our experience to the fires which threatened God-fearing Shadrach, Meshach and Abednego, of whom it was written:- *the fire had not had any power over the bodies of those men; the hair of their heads was not singed, their mantles were not harmed, and no smell of fire had come upon them,* (Daniel 3:27) *because God delivered His servants who trusted in Him.* (Daniel 3:28)

In heaven, we read again *the sun shall not strike them nor any scorching heat.* Why is this so? Well let us explain the nature of hell's fire somewhat more. The Bible often uses fire to symbolise the wrath of God - His righteous anger, indignation and holy revulsion against sin. *Who can stand before His indignation? Who can endure the heat of His anger? His wrath is poured out like fire, and the rocks are broken asunder by Him.* (Nahum 1:6) Indeed, the less popular truth about God is that *Our God is a consuming fire.* (Hebrews 12:29) Way back in the time of Abraham, this fact was witnessed most forcefully in the towns of Sodom and Gomorrah. *There the Lord rained on Sodom and Gomorrah brimstone and fire from the Lord out of heaven.* (Genesis 19:24) He had no choice but to do this because *the outcry against Sodom and Gomorrah is great and their sin is very grave.* (Genesis 18:20) That was in the past; but we should take note that *I the Lord do not change.* (Malachi 3:6) He is still holy, and must still judge sin and unrepentant sinners - despite the fact that some of the cities in modern day Great Britain make Sodom and Gommorah look rather tame. *The heavens and earth that now exist have been stored for fire, being kept until the day of judgement and destruction of ungodly men.* (2 Peter 3:7) The Day is coming *when the Lord Jesus is revealed from heaven with His mighty angels in flaming fire, inflicting vengeance upon those who do not know God and upon those who do not obey the Gospel of our Lord Jesus.* (2 Thessalonians 1:7)

The believer, however, can rejoice that he will have to suffer no such judgement of fire. Why not? Because of Christ. A fuller answer can be gleaned from a verse of a matchless Christian hymn:-

> *Jehovah bade His sword awake*
> *O Christ it woke 'gainst Thee*
> *Thy blood the flaming sword must slake*
> *Thy heart its sheath must be*
> *All for my sake, my peace to make*
> *Now sleeps that sword for me.*

The good news is that the believer has been saved from God's judgement of fire, because His sins have already been judged in Christ. It is the blood of Jesus that has put out the flames of God's wrath for all who trust in Him. The Bible uses the word 'propitiation' to explain this most blessed of facts. 'To propitiate' means 'to turn away wrath, to appease, to render propitious.' It is written of Jesus that *He is the propitiation for our sins.* (1 John 2:2) And it is this which perhaps takes us to the 'heart of the heart' of the Gospel more than anything else.

THE PARDON OF GUILT

The essence of the Christian Gospel is that *Christ died for our sins.* (1 Corinthians 15:3) On the Cross, Christ suffered the righteous punishment and wrath of Almighty God for sins not His Own. *He was put to death for our trespasses.* (Romans 4:25) The Scriptures assure us that by His substitutionary death on the Cross for our sins, Christ has pacified the wrath of God. This is the

Christian Gospel - nothing more, nothing less and nothing else. It is this alone which gives the believer the inner assurance of his eternal security that *There is therefore now no condemnation to those who are in Christ Jesus.* (Romans 8:1) Let us have a verse from another well known Christian hymn:-

Bearing shame and scoffing rude
In my place condemned He stood
Sealed my pardon with His blood
Hallelujah! What a Saviour!

THE PEACE OF GRACE

So we glimpse something of the the Divine security of heaven; a security wrought on Calvary's cross, where Christ went through the fires of judgement to deliver the believer from hell's fires to the Land where *the sun shall not strike them, nor any scorching heat.* Revelation informs us that there is actually no sun in heaven. How then can there be light and life there, as a biologist would tell us that all life and light eminates ultimately from the sun, and that everything would soon die if the sun stopped shining? The answer is that *the city has no need of sun or moon to shine upon it for the glory of God is its light and its lamp is the Lamb.* (Revelation 21:23) *God is light* (1 John 1:5) and it was He Who *made the two great lights, the greater light to rule the day and the lesser light to rule the night.* (Genesis 1:16) And His first act of creation was to say *'Let there be light'* and there was light. (Genesis 1:3)

This is the God Who in Christ has provided such a great salvation for all who believe. Those who believe in

Christ will one day enjoy God's security forever, and dwell with Him in the land of endless day, basking in the safety of His love and light for all eternity. Then we will know indeed that absolutely no harsh forces at all *will be able to separate us from the love of God in Christ Jesus our Lord.* (Romans 8:39)

CHAPTER EIGHT

The Divine Shepherd of Heaven

For the Lamb in the midst of the throne will be their shepherd. (Revelation 7:17)

THE SHEPHERD CELESTIAL

What a paradox we have here! The verse tells us that the same Lamb Who is intimately related to God in royal state is also a shepherd. The roles of Lamb and Shepherd would appear to be contradictory, but as both are true of Christ, paradoxically would be a better description.

Our text tells us that the Lamb is the Shepherd and the Shepherd is the Lamb! Truth, when considering the glorious person of Christ, is often a case not so much of 'either/or' but 'both/and.' For example, the Bible makes it crystal clear that Jesus Christ is both fully human and fully divine yet One person - *For in Him the whole fullness of deity dwells bodily.* (Colossians 2:9) The Bible also tells us of Jesus that This Man receives sinners and eats with them, (Luke 15:2) but yet is equally adament that Jesus is *holy, blameless, unstained, separated from sinners.* (Hebrews 7:26) Another paradox can be seen by comparing the Jesus' invitation which said *If any one thirst, let him come to Me and drink,* (John 7:37) with the words *I thirst* (John 19:28) which He uttered on the Cross. Further examples of such paradoxes could be given, not the least of which is the paradoxical truth that Jesus, the immortal God and Second Person of the Trinity actually died. ''Tis mystery all, the immortal dies,' wrote Wesley - and equally mysterious is the fact that His death brings us life and His pains bring us pardon. 'Who can explore His strange design?'

From our study of Church history, we can see that much error and heresy has resulted from emphasising one polarity of the truth about Christ at the expense and detriment of the other. We find that in the Christian Faith, truth is not so much in one extreme or the other extreme but in both extremes! This is so in the truth we are considering now, that the Lamb is also the Shepherd. Jesus is the Divine Shepherd of heaven.

THE SCRIPTURE CONNECTION

The shepherd theme runs throughout the Bible, and this is not surprising when we consider that much of it was written in an agricultural, pastoral setting. Many people's favourite Psalm begins *The Lord is my shepherd, I shall not want.* (Psalm 23:1) Less well known is the description of God in Isaiah 41:11, *He will feed His flock like a shepherd, He will gather the lambs in His arms, He will carry them in His bosom, and gently lead those that are with young.* Israel even used to celebrate this fact in song - *He is our God, and we are the people of His pasture and the sheep of His hand.* (Psalm 95:7)

THE SHEPHERDIC CALLING

Some of Israel's greatest leaders were shepherds before they moved on to higher things. *Moses was keeping the flock of his father-in-law, Jethro when the angel of the Lord appeared to him in a flame of fire out of the midst of a bush,* (Exodus 3:1,2) and called and commissioned Moses to lead the people of Israel out of slavery in Egypt. *Thou didst lead Thy people like a flock by the hand of Moses and Aaron.* (Psalm 77:20)

David was Israel's greatest king. Yet before Samuel anointed David, thus setting him apart for this high office, we see David at his normal occupation:- *behold he is keeping the sheep.* (1 Samuel 16:11) Indeed, *He chose David His servant, and took him from the sheepfolds; from tending the ewes that had young He brought him to be shepherd of Jacob His people, of Israel His inheritance.* (Psalm 78:70,71)

Perhaps the hint here, considering the lives and backgrounds of both Moses and David, is that before one can pastor and lead God's people, one has first of all to know God's Own personal, pastoral care in ones' own life and experience. Moses and David knew God as their Shepherd before they became His under-shepherds. They both knew God as their Shepherd, and proved Him to be so out in the lonely, barren wilderness, where every artificial prop of man dies. Knowing God as their Shepherd equipped and qualified them to shepherd God's people.

THE SCANDALOUS CONDITION

Alas, however, Scripture does not hide from us the faults and failings of Israel's earthly shepherds. Moses murdered a man, lost his temper and forfeited his right to enter into the promised land. David committed adultery, connived a murder to try and cover it up, and at one time was guilty of numbering the people - guilty because it suggested that his faith was more in military might than in the Might of God Almighty.

As time went on, the leadership of Israel's earthly shepherds and leaders degenerated further. In Ezekiel 34 we read of the Divine indictment against such 'shepherds.' "*Ho, shepherds of Israel who have been feeding yourselves! Should not shepherds feed the sheep.*" (Ezekiel 34:2) *Thus says the Lord God,"Behold, I am against the shepherds.*" (Ezekiel 34:10)

Yet all was not lost. In His long-suffering goodness, God promised that in the future a Good Shepherd of His Own choosing would come. The promise went "*I will set up over them one shepherd, My servant David, and He will feed them: He shall feed them and be their shepherd,*" (Ezekiel 34:23) - another of the promises superabundantly fulfilled in Jesus, the One Who stated *I am the Good Shepherd.* (John 10:11) This is the Shepherd Who really cares for His sheep. *When He saw the crowds, He had compassion for them, because they were harassed and helpless, like sheep without a shepherd.* (Matthew 9:36) This is the Shepherd in Whose company and care the Christian will abide for all eternity. It is to this Shepherd, the Divine Shepherd of heaven, that we will now turn and consider just some aspects of His multi-faceted pastoral ministry.

THE SHEPHERD CHRIST

The Divine Shepherd of heaven is the same One Who said here on earth, *I am the Good Shepherd.* (John 10:11)

The Lion Handbook to the Bible comments:- 'The shepherd was a familiar figure in Palestine. He spent much of his life with his flock. His own sheep knew and responded to his voice (c.f. *I am the Good Shepherd; I know My own and My own know Me. John 10:14... My sheep hear My voice and I know them and follow them and they follow Me.* (John 10:27) He led (not drove) them to fresh grazing and guarded them from wild animals by lying across the entrance to the sheepfold at night, so becoming its 'door.' In the Old Testament God is often called the Shepherd of Israel (as we have seen, c.f. Psalm 80:1) and His chosen leaders are also the nation's shepherds. Now Jesus chooses to describe Himself as the true shepherd. The phrase sums up so much: the close, personal relationship between Himself and each of His followers; the absolute security we have in Him; His leadership and guidance; His constant company; His unfailing care; His sacrificial love.'

It is this Shepherd Who literally loved us to death. It is this Shepherd in Whose company we will delight for all eternity if we have been saved by His grace here in this life. Let us now consider just four aspects of our Good Shepherd's manifold ministry. We will see what the Bible has to say about:- 1. His saving care 2. His sacrificial cross 3. His succouring concern and 4. His second coming.

1. THE SAVING CARE OF THE GRACIOUS SHEPHERD

Jesus stated *The Son of Man came to seek and to save the lost.* (Luke 19:10) And Jesus once depicted this in parabolic form, using the imagery of a shepherd looking for one of his lost sheep:- *What man of you, having a hundred sheep, if he has lost one of them, does not leave the ninety-nine in the wilderness, and go after the one which is lost until he finds it? And when he has found it, he lays it on his shoulders rejoicing. And when he comes home, he calls together his friends and his neighbours saying to them, 'Rejoice with me for I have found my sheep which was lost.' Just so, I tell you, there will be more joy in heaven over one sinner who repents than over ninety-nine righteous persons who need no repentance.* (Luke 15: 4-7)

Jesus left His home in glory to rescue His 'lost sheep' here on earth. It was an act of infinite grace. He stooped so low to lift us so high. He left heaven for earth so that we might leave earth for heaven; He tasted Perdition in time so that we might have Paradise for all eternity. The saving care of the gracious Shepherd!

> *None of the ransomed ever knew*
> *how deep were the waters crossed*
> *Nor how dark was the night that the Lord passed*
> *through*
> *Ere He found His sheep that was lost*
> *Out in the desert He heart its cry*
> *sick and helpless and ready to die*

But how exactly did the Shepherd rescue His sheep? By:-

2. THE SACRIFICIAL CROSS OF THE GIVING SHEPHERD

We only half quoted John 10:11 earlier. The complete verse reads:- *I am the Good Shepherd. The Good Shep-*

herd lays down His life for the sheep. Jesus did indeed give His life for His sheep - just as the prophet had predicted years earlier, *Awake, O sword, against My Shepherd,... Strike the Shepherd, that the sheep may be scattered...* (Zechariah 13:7, c.f. Matthew 26:31 and Mark 14:27.)

The sacrificial Cross of the giving Shepherd is the heart of the New Testament's message. *Christ died for our sins.* (1 Corinthians 15:3) *He was put to death for our trespasses,* (Romans 4:25.) The sacrificial Cross of the giving Shepherd is also the focus and theme of heaven's praise, as we have already seen. Jesus is the Shepherd and the Lamb, He is the Priest and the Victim. *He has appeared once for all at the end of the age to put away sin by the sacrifice of Himself.* (Hebrews 9:26)

Jesus once said to His disciples *Greater love has no man than this, that a man lay down his life for his friends.* (John 16:13) But Jesus did more. He layed down His life for His enemies. *God shows His love for us in that while we were yet sinners Christ died for us.* (Romans 5:8).... *while we were enemies we were reconciled to God by the death of His Son..* (Romans 5:10) Such is the grace of the Good Shepherd Who gave Himself for His undeserving and ill-deserving sheep.

> *Loving Shepherd, Thou didst give*
> *Thine Own life that I might live*
> *May I love Thee day by day*
> *Gladly Thy sweet will obey.*

The Cross refers to the finished work of the Good Shepherd Who said *It is finished,* (John 19:30) when He gave up His life. We move on now though to what may

be termed the 'unfinished work' of Christ our Shepherd
- the work He continues to do:-

3. THE SUCCOURING CONCERN OF THE
   GUARDIAN SHEPHERD

In his later years, Peter the fisherman was well
established as Peter the Pastor. As a leader of the Church
he took it upon himself to write to encourage his fellow
Pastors. Note his exhortation to *Tend the flock of God
that is your charge... being examples to the flock.* (1 Peter
5:2,3) Yet Peter knew that any authority he had was
merely a delegated authority, as he himself was an
under-shepherd, under the supreme authority and care of
Christ, the Chief Shepherd. So he reminded the Christian flock to whom he was writing *...you were straying
like sheep, but have now returned to the Shepherd and
Guardian of your souls.* (1 Peter 2:25) The Shepherd
Who gave His life for the sheep still lives to keep His
sheep. Jesus said of them *I give them eternal life, and
they shall never perish and no one shall snatch them out
of My hand.* (John 10:28) There we see the total security
of the sheep under the succouring concern and safe
keeping of the Shepherd Christ, the Shepherd Who leads
us and feeds us and guards us and guides us.

*Like a Shepherd, Jesus will guard His children
In His arms He carries them all day long*

and those under His tender authority will surely be able
to testify, T*he Lord is my shepherd, I shall not want.*
(Psalm 23:1)
Finally, the New Testament teaches us, not only about

the past and present ministries of the good, gracious, guardian Shepherd, but also something about His promised glory in the future:-

4. THE SECOND COMING OF THE GLORIOUS SHEPHERD

Looking ahead, under the inspiration of the Holy Spirit, Peter penned:- *when the Chief Shepherd is manifested you will obtain the unfading crown of glory.* (1 Peter 5:4) And what a glorious day it will be, when Jesus fulfils the promise He made when He said *I will come again and take you to Myself, that where I am you may be also.* (John 14:3)

THE SURE CONDITION

And so we have been considering the peerless Divine Shepherd of heaven. This is the Shepherd Whose delightful company the Christian will enjoy for all eternity, either way, whether the Lord comes or calls. *For the Lamb in the midst of the throne will be their shepherd.* (Revelation 7:17) And the famous shepherd Psalm which begins *The Lord is my shepherd,* (Psalm 23:1) ends with the glad certainty *And I shall dwell in the house of the Lord forever.* (Psalm 23:6) - and the Christian surely shall!

> *And so through all the length of days*
> *Thy goodness faileth never*
> *Good Shepherd, I will sing Thy praise*
> *Within Thy house for ever.*

CHAPTER NINE

The Divine Spring of Heaven

And He will guide them to springs of living water.
(Revelation 7:17)

THE SCRIPTURE DOCTRINE

The Bible is a wet Book! On its opening pages we read *A river flowed out of Eden to water the garden, and there it divided and became four rivers,* (Genesis 2:10) whilst its last chapter opens *Then he showed me the river of the water of life, bright as crystal, flowing from the throne of God and of the Lamb.* (Revelation 22:1) Then at the Bible's focal point - the death of Christ on the Cross to save sinners - we read *one of the soldiers pierced His side with a spear, and at once there came out blood and water.* (John 19:34)

Water is essential for both physical and spiritual life. The Bible often uses the universal commodity of water as a symbol of eternal life and salvation. *With joy you will draw water from the wells of salvation.* (Isaiah 12:3) In heaven, our text for this chapter tells us that the Lord Jesus *will guide them to springs of living water.* There we have the Divine spring of heaven, symbolising the

ultimate source and origin of all spiritual life and blessing. *Thou makest springs gush forth in the valleys; they
flow between the hills.* (Psalm 104:10)

> *See from Zion's sacred mountain*
> *Streams of living water flow*
> *God has opened there a fountain*
> *That supplies the plains below*
> *They are blessed, ever blessed*
> *Who its sovereign virtues know.*

PHYSICAL THIRST : SPIRITUAL THIRST

Water is essential for physical/biological life. The
thirst mechanism which our Creator gave us ensures that
we maintain our water balance and keep our body cells
in a state of homeostasis. The author well remembers the
disruption which ensued at a certain office in which he
once worked whenever the tea break was delayed! Also,
the necessity of water was enforced on him through his
interest in long-distance running. Dehydration can be a
serious problem when running a 26 mile marathon on a
hot day. Race organisers thus ensure drinking stations
every five miles or so.

Less anecdotally, 'Water is absolutely essential for life
as it forms nearly a quarter of body weight. It forms all
the body fluids and is necessary for the formation of the
secretions of the glands. The amount of water in the body
is about 45 litres. 30 litres are present inside the cells and
15 litres lie outside as extra cellular fluid which is the
tissue fluid and the plasma. If the body is depleted of
fluid the signs and symptoms of dehydration
occur."(J.Riddle. Anatomy and Physiology as Applied

to Nursing; Churchill Livingstone; 1985; page 99)

Thirst is very unpleasant. When the Lord Jesus said *I thirst* (John 19:28) as He hung on the Cross in the heat of the day, having lost much blood, whatever spiritual interpretation we may give to His words, at their base level they show that Jesus knows what it is like to be human. He certainly felt physical pain and agonising discomfort when He took upon Himself our flesh two thousand years ago.

THE SINNER'S DESIRE

Water is also essential for spiritual life. Everyone knows what it is like to be physically thirsty, but there is an equally real phenomenon of sprriitual thirst too; and we all have this spiritual thirst owing to our being made in the image of God. Spiritual thirst is less tangible than physical thirst, as it is also less articulate and unconscious in most people. Nevertheless, spiritual thirst is still there. The Psalmist spoke for Everyman when he wrote *As a hart longs for flowing streams, so longs my soul for Thee O God. My soul thirsts for God, for the living God. When shall I come and behold the face of God?* (Psalm 42:1,2)

Spiritual thirst is insatiable until it is quenched by God Himself with God Himself. This being said however, it is surprising to see that many people seek 'soul satisfaction' in anything and everything other than the God and Father of our Lord Jesus Christ. Spiritual substitutes abound, be this in the form of a human relationship, exciting sport or hobby, work, wealth, status, sex, drugs, alchohol, entertainment and much much else. But do these satisfy? The evidence proclaims that they do not, as the world today is as restless and as dissatisfied as it has ever been. The Bible gives us the Divine verdict on all this:- *My people have committed two evils: they have forsaken Me the fountain of living water, and hewed out cisterns for themselves, broken cisterns that can hold no water.* (Jeremiah 2:13) We may contrast this Divine condemnation though with a Divine invitation elsewhere:- *Ho, every one who thirsts, come to the waters... Hearken diligently to Me... Incline your ear and come to Me...* (Isaiah 55:1-3)

THE SINISTER DEARTH

The nature of spiritual thirst can perhaps be clarified by considering the most extreme case of this undesirable state. Hell, amongst other things, is having an agonising, intense and raging thirst for God, but a thirst which cannot or never will be satisfied. Hell is thus an endless spiritual thirst. The rich man who went to hell in Jesus' parable is described as *in Hades, being in torment,* (Luke 16:23) and in his agony he cried out *Father Abraham, have mercy upon me, and send Lazarus to dip the end of his finger in water and cool my tongue; for I am in anguish in this flame.* (Luke 16:24)

Lest we are in any doubt concerning hell as a state and place of spiritual thirst, let us consider again some of the suffering which Jesus underwent on the Cross, to save the sinner from a thirsty hell. On that most cruel of gallows, *For our sake He made Him to be sin Who knew no sin,* (2 Corinthians 5:21) as *God, sending His Own Son in the likeness of sinful flesh and for sin, He condemned sin in the flesh.* (Romans 8:3) In Christ, God judged our sins; He literally bore the wrath of God in the sinner's place. Christ actually tasted hell for us so we may go to heaven. Hell is being forsaken by God, and on the Cross Christ was forsaken by God so that He cried out *My God My God why hast Thou forsaken Me?* (Matthew 27:46) We have said that hell is having a thirst for God that cannot be quenched; thus on the Cross Jesus cried *I thirst*. (John 19:28) If we need a reminder of the severity of hell then, all we have to do is take a look at the Cross of Christ. Yet His hell is our heaven; He thirsted so that we may never thirst. His death in our place on the Cross for our sins is the heart of the Gospel, to be preached and embraced. *Like cold water to a thirsty soul, so is good news from a far country.* (Proverbs 25:25)

THE SUPPLY DIVINE

In Isaiah 35:6,7 we read *Waters shall break forth in the wilderness, and streams in the desert; the burning sand shall become a pool, and the thirsty ground springs of water.*

God promises to all who trust in Him that they will never thirst as they go through this dry, earthly wilderness, onwards and upwards to their heavenly glory. The Psalmist wrote *Blessed are the men whose strength is in Thee, in whose heart are the highways to Zion. As they go through the valley of Baca they make it a place of springs; the early rain also covers it with pools.* (Psalm 84:5,6) And the truly happy man of the first Psalm whose delight is in the law of the Lord is described significantly as *like a tree planted by streams of water, that yields its fruit in its season and its leaf does not wither.* (Psalm 1:2,3)

The ultimate source of all physical and spiritual life is God Himself. He is the only truly independant Being, and we are completely dependant on Him. He is the One Who abundantly provides for all our needs, and this is especially so concerning the need which our parched, thirsty, dry and shrivelled souls have for life-giving water. *He leads me beside still waters,* (Psalm 23:2) wrote David in the shepherd Psalm, (and as a side-point, from our background we know that sheep would be too frightened to drink fast, rushing water, no matter how thirsty they were.)

Another promise of God through the prophet Isaiah reads *I will pour water on the thirsty land and streams on the dry ground; I will pour My Spirit upon your descendants, and My blessing on your offspring.* (Isaiah 44:3) As this promise, as in all God's promises (see 2 Corinthians 1:20) found its fulfilment in Jesus, we turn now to see what Jesus had to say on our topic of water to quench the spiritual thirst of man. Jesus, by His Holy Spirit, provides abundantly for both personal and national revival and transformation in people and places which would otherwise remain spiritually dead and dry.

THE SAVIOUR'S DECLARATIONS

Tired and thirsty, Jesus once sat down by a well, during the course of His earthly ministry, when, *There came a woman of Samaria to draw water.* (John 4:7) This woman was as despised nationally as she was depraved personally, but Jesus did not turn her away, rather He made a promise to her - not to mention to every sinner aware of their need. He declared, *whoever drinks of the water that I shall give Him will never thirst; the water*

88

*that I shall give him will become in him a spring of water,
welling up to eternal life.* (John 4:14)

> *Poor, sinful, fainting souls
> Are freely welcome here
> Salvation, like a river rolls
> Abundant, free and clear.*

The next time that Jesus made such a declaration was
on a public not a private occasion - in front of perhaps
several thousand people. It was the Feast of the Taber-
nacles in Jerusalem, and Jesus was there. On the last day
of the feast, an elaborate ceremony was carried out by
the priest. To a cry of 'Lord, give us rain,' (to ensure that
farmers could plough their fields after the summer's
hardening effect on the ground) and "Lord, send us
salvation," the priest drew a golden pitcher of water
from the pool of Siloam. Then, returning to the Temple,
with great ceremony, he poured the water out upon the
horns of the great altar. At that exact moment Jesus stood
up and proclaimed, *'If any one thirst, let him come to Me
and drink. He who believes in Me, as the Scripture has
said 'Out of his heart shall flow rivers of living water.''*
(John 7:37) Both the timing and the immediate context
of the Saviour's declaration here make it especially
meaningful. John also gives us the inspired explanation
in his commentary *Now this He said about the Holy
Spirit, which those who believed in Him were to receive.*
(John 7:39)

THE SUPREME DELIGHT

In heaven we will still have the desire for fellowship
with God, and this desire will be totally satisfied in a way

only just glimpsed on earth, where so much within us and without us seeks to draw us away from God. We are assured from our opening verse, that in heaven *He will guide them to springs of living water.* Our spiritual thirst will then be delightfully, delectably and Divinely quenched forever!

THE SUPERNAL DRINK

Incase any reader reading these words has not as yet experienced the truth of the words *O taste and see that the Lord is good! Happy is the man who takes refuge in Him,* (Psalm 34:8) and has only just realised the unsatisfied thirst which their soul has, be assured that Jesus' offer of living water for thirsty souls still stands, even now. Almost the very last verse of the Bible contains a promise and invitation which proves that this is so. *Let him who is thirsty come, let him who desires take the water of life without price.* (Revelation 22:17)

> *I heard the voice of Jesus say*
> *Behold I freely give*
> *The living water thirsty one*
> *Stoop down and drink and live*
> *I came to Jesus and I drank*
> *of that life-giving stream*
> *My thirst was quenched, my soul revived*
> *And now I live in Him.*

CHAPTER TEN

The Divine Sensitivity of Heaven

God will wipe away every tear from their eyes.
(Revelation 7:17)

INTRODUCTION

Tears are part and parcel of life on earth. We would rather shy away from discussing the unpleasant fact of tears, but that would not make tears themselves go away. Earthly life is a mysterious mixture of tears and smiles, sorrows and joys.

There will be no more tears in heaven! Our text assures us that *God will wipe away every tear from their eyes.*

> *There'll be a glad glad tomorrow*
> *in the sweet sweet bye and bye*
> *There'll be no crying or sorrow*
> *every tear drop will be dry*

The text shows us the Divine sensitivity of heaven. The eye is one of the most delicate organs of the human body, and here we see that the great God Who is mighty enough to speak this vast universe into existence is nevertheless tender enough to gently wipe away all the tears out of the eyes of His children. Such is our God! *He heals the brokenhearted, and binds up their wounds. He determines the number of the stars, He gives to all of them their names.* (Psalm 147:3,4)

Recalling the original context in which Revelation was written, i.e. a letter to encourage the persecuted Church, 'words like these must have sounded as a Divine music in the ears of the persecuted. God will comfort as a mother comforts.' (G.B. Wilson) These words have also been music to the ears of Christians ever since, as we walk through the vale of tears of this life. Yet in heaven, our glad testimony will be, *..Thou hast delivered my soul from death, my eyes from tears, my feet from stumbling.* (Psalm 116:8)

1. TEARS : THEIR CONSTERNATION

My tears have been my food day and night, (Psalm 42:3) wrote the Psalmist, and not one of us will have any difficulty in relating to his words. Tears are an unpleasant fact of life in an imperfect world and they are with us from infancy until old age. Tears are no respecter of persons; at some time everyone will taste their bitter, salty flavour, whether religious or irreligious, rich or poor, Protestant or Catholic.

When we are in extreme physical or emotional pain, we cry. Whilst tears have some physiological basis, (all animals have tear-ducts to keep their eyes lubricated) tears are more especially the saline expression of the human soul. Animals may show signs of distress, but they do not weep. We do.

Writing from this trouble-torn city of Belfast, one wonders just how many tears have been shed here since 'the troubles' began in 1969. Behind every bombing and maiming there is a human tragedy. Every man killed is someone's son, father, husband or boyfriend. Recently, the writer witnessed an elderly lady whose childhood home had been completely gutted, along with her precious and irreplacable personal possessions. All had been destroyed in a bomb-blast that lasted a split second. The physical, psychological and emotional devastation of this lovely but tragic Province just cannot be measured. The tears shed in Ulster over the last twenty years or so would surely fill a large swimming pool - and the tears shed in the whole world over the last two thousand years would surely fill a large lake.

Each of us will shed some tears in our life time - few or many, depending on how many God considers we are able to bear, *For He knows our frame...* (Psalm 103:14) *and He will not let you be tempted beyond your strength.* (1 Corinthians 10:13) Tears express the deepest longings of the human soul in a chemical solution. They are both a subject and an experience which we would rather avoid - so how heartening then, for the Christian to know that God is the Almighty tear-dryer as God *will wipe away tears from all faces.* (Isaiah 25:8)

2. TEARS : THEIR CONSIDERATION

The causes of tears are many. Tears come upon us when we reach the brink and stand dangerously near to the edge of extremity. Tears may result from failure, frustration, dashed hopes, broken dreams, a broken relationship, disappointment, depression or indeed any incident or circumstance which threatens us and drives us to despair. The tear-tap is sometimes turned on very suddenly, when tears were least expected:- a family ride out in the car suddenly ruined by an accident; a routine check-up at the Doctors' unexpectedly revealing a fatal illness; an innocent looking envelope containing a redundancy note ...... We all have unpleasant examples which we could give.

Bereavement is perhaps the classic example of a great tear manufacturer. What of the sense of hopelessness and helplessness on hearing the news of a loved ones' terminal illness? The emotional pain of weakening earthly ties as heaven's ties are strengthened - not to mention the paralysing sense of loss at marching slowly and solemnly behind a dear one's coffin? All these will lead even the most hardened to betray his humanity and give liquid expression to his soul.

i. The Apostle Peter

The Apostle Peter had, as we say, 'a thick skin.' As a Galilean fisherman by trade, he was used to working in hard, rugged conditions, and would have had the physical frame adapted to it. Galilean fishermen, then as now, are notoriously rough, tough and even coarse. But the Bible tells us of a time when *Peter went out and wept bitterly*. (Luke 22:62) I have underlined that word 'bitterly.' Tears are a bitter experience, and the cause of Peter's bitter tears were the same as ours - he had failed his Master. In an act of cowardice, he had sworn that he had never even known the lovliest Friend he had ever had. There is nothing like failure to bring us down. Luke records that *the Lord turned and looked at Peter*. (Luke 22:61) What poignant words those are; it is no wonder that Peter wept. Perhaps he feared that his friendship with Jesus was irrepairable; broken relationships, then as now, are a particular producer of floods of tears. But what Peter did not know then, we know now, (see John 21:15-19.) In an act of sheer grace, the risen Lord personally restored Peter to Himself - just as He does with us when we fail Him, hurt Him and deny Him. *If we confess our sins He is faithful and just and will forgive our sins and cleanse us from all unrighteousness.* (1 John 1:9)

ii. The Awful Perdition

In previous chapters we saw how hell is the complete opposite and antithesis to heaven, and this has heightened heaven's delights as well us underlining hell's damnation. Our topic here, that of there being no tears in heaven, follows suit, as according to Jesus the 'outer darkness' of hell is where *men will weep and gnash their teeth.* (Matthew 8:12) The Christian is assured from the Word of God that one day God will wipe away all his tears - but the unbeliever will be denied such a blessedness, however tear-free his existence in this life may be. Hell is eternal remorse. Hell is eternal weeping. How imperative then it is to believe in Jesus in this life. Jesus died to save us from hell's tears. Jesus tasted hell on the Cross so that whoever believes in Him may enjoy eternal life both now and forever. Hell is characterised by crying and weeping. Heaven is characterised by a chorus of worship. When this life is over, there will be no way of escape from one side to the other as *a great chasm has been fixed, in order that those who would pass from here to you may not be able, and none may pass from there to us.* (Luke 16:26) This is the believer's eternal delight; this is the unbeliever's eternal damnation. So the message in this life is still urgent: *Believe in the Lord Jesus and you will be saved* (Acts 16:31) - saved from hell, saved from tears.

3. TEARS : THEIR CONSOLATION

Without the aid of the Word of God, tears would seem to be totally senseless and just an agonising perplexity. The Bible however sheds light on the subject of tears, and through our tears lets us see a rainbow of glory. Yet again *Thy Word is a light to my feet and a lamp to my path.* (Psalm 119:105) We may even suggest that tears are for our ultimate betterment rather than for our bitterment, as we learn lessons in the University of Weeping that just cannot be learned in any other way. But does God really bring blessing from buffeting? Ponder the following:-

a. God understands our tears

In Jesus Christ, God became Man; the incarnation is one of the stupendous fundamentals of *the Faith which was once for all delivered to the saints.* (Jude 3) The incarnation shows that our God is not some distant Deity, far removed from our troubles, trials and tears. Far from it. *The Word became flesh and dwelt among us.* (John 1:14) Our God, in Jesus Christ, knows exactly what it is like to be human. Jesus was immune from sin but not from tears. The shortest verse in the Bible reads *Jesus wept.* (John 11:35)

It is so easy for us to feel isolated and alone in our tears, and in a sense we are, as we are all unique, and our circumstances are different and we react to our different circumstances in different ways. There is no loneliness like the loneliness of private tears, yet even here, God has promised *I will never fail you nor forsake you.*

(Hebrews 13:5) Fear, shame and the fear of being ashamed usually enable us to put on a bold public face - but in private we lose all such inhibitions. We may recall at such dire moments that *we have not a high priest Who is unable to sympathise with our weaknesses,* (Hebrews 4:14) since Jesus Himself knows what it is like to cry. *Jesus wept.* (John 11:35) He was no stranger to the all too human phenomenon of shedding tears - even though He was very God of very God.

b. God knows our tears

Put Thou my tears in a bottle, (Psalm 56:8) cried out the Psalmist in anguish to God - and such tear bottles, unusual as they sound, can still be seen in the middle east (and Western Jewish communities) today.

The Christian may be sure that his tears are measured in God's bottle, and that not one of his tears of anguish and distress will drop without his heavenly Father's notice. God our Father is everywhere and sees all things, and in a way which our finite minds can never fathom, He has actually ordained all things for our benefit - even those events which cause us to shed buckets of tears. *We know that in everything God works for good with those who love Him.* (Romans 8:28)

What a comfort for the tearful child of God is Isaiah 38:5. *Thus says the Lord... I have heard your prayer, I HAVE SEEN YOUR TEARS.* Jesus assures us that *even the hairs of your head are all numbered,* (Luke 12:7) so we can be absolutely certain that no matter how deep our pit is, and even though we may be forgotten by men and forsaken by friends, we are still remembered by God! *You will not be forgotten by Me,* (Isaiah 44:21) says the Lord.

c. God uses our tears

The Arabs have a proverb 'No rain makes a desert.' Of course we would all rather a tear-free existence, but would such an existence here on earth necessarily be the best for us? Imagine a pain and sickness-free body; full and satisfying employment; smooth, unbroken relationships; no financial worries.... Imagine never experiencing failure, fatigue and frustration. Imagine ... being free from whatever it is that causes you tears. Such an existence would be perilous! We would be in danger of forgetting God, (see Deuteronomy 8:11-14) and forgetting "I need Thee every hour." Our desire for heaven would become blunt, and - our commonwealth is in heaven (Philippians 3:20) - as we would be quite happy for an eternal existence on earth, if it were possible. Tears bring us to our senses. In our tears, we realise that we are creatures, totally dependant on our Creator, as He holds our life and breath in the palm of His hand, (c.f. Psalm 31:15 and Daniel 5:23) How frail and fickle we are! How we need to be anchored to God our Rock. Man's extremity is God's opportunity; He brings us down to lift us up. Psalm 34:18 *The Lord is near to the broken-hearted, and saves the crushed in spirit.* In our insufficiency we are cast on His all-sufficiency. Amidst our tears, when all our well-plotted plans are in pieces, we realise afresh the truth of Jesus' words *apart from Me you can do nothing.* (John 15:5)

d. God waters our prayers by tears

The sacrifice acceptable to God is a broken spirit; a broken and contrite heart, O God, Thou wilt not despise. (Psalm 51:17)

Tears give reality to our prayers. Much of our life is spent behind a facade, putting on an act, assuming a role, fooling others, maybe even fooling ourselves. How easy it is to play the athlete, the businessman, the intellectual, the comedian or even the evangelical. Tears however rub off all such external paint and reveal our real selves. It is a sad fact that even our prayers can have an air of unreality about them. They can become mechanical, poetic and perfunctory. We can get into a rut of 'saying our prayers' in private or 'doing the prayers' in public.

In the vale of tears however, we are brought back to reality with a bump. Here we are forced to believe in the supernatural efficacy of prayer, having had all natural props knocked away from us. Prayerful tears and tearful prayers have a power about them. They are prayers from the heart and not just the lips. Prayer here is not just 'going through the motions' but a laying hold on Omnipotence. (c.f. Jacob at Peniel, Genesis 32)

e. God tenderises by our tears

Finally, under our heading of the consolation of tears, we may suggest that God uses tears to teach us the much needed grace of sympathy and tenderness towards others. Tears make us more careful as well as more prayerful. It is so easy to cause a fellow human being a needless hurt by our blase, flippant behaviour - unaware that they may be aching inside. Tears put a clamp on such unthinking behaviour and make us into a channel of Divine comfort.

In our tears, God comforts us to make us comforters. He is indeed *the Father of mercies and God of all comfort, Who comforts us in all our affliction, so that we may be able to comfort those who are in any affliction with the comfort with which we ourselves are comforted by God.* (2 Corinthians 1:4)

4. TEARS : THEIR CONCLUSION

The picture so far has been realistic but gloomy: we live in a tearful world, and if we have so far been spared their bitter, salty tang, we are the exception that proves the rule.

The prospect for the believer however, inspite of present tears, is exceedingly bright - as bright as the promises of the *God Who never lies.* (Titus 1:2) Indelibly engraved in God's Word is His promise that one day He is going to undertake a personal action on our behalf. Returning to our opening text, *God will wipe away every tear from their eyes.* (Revelation 7:17) As the Apostle Paul, no stranger to tears himself (see 2 Corinthians 2:4) reminded the Corinthians, *this slight momentary affliction is preparing for us an eternal weight of glory beyond comparison.* (2 Corinthians 4:17) On a similar vein, A.W.Pink once said, 'One breath of Paradise will extinguish all the adverse winds of earth.' Yes. The joys of heaven will more than super-abundantly compensate us for all the tears we may have shed here on earth.

5. TEARS : THEIR CRUCIFIXION

Finally, we ask the question 'Is anything worse than tears?' The answer is 'Yes,' if we think Biblically. Biblically, sin is worse than tears as sin is the ultimate cause of all tears and sorrow. But when Christ was crucified *He Himself bore our sins in His body on the tree.* (1 Peter 2:24) and it is because of the Cross of Jesus that God is able to wipe away our tears - fully, finally and forever! On the Cross, Jesus, the sinless One took upon Himself all our sins and God's just punishment upon them so that whoever believes in Him may be saved from sin's condemnation in a tearful hell. It is no wonder then, that in Gethsemane, in contemplation of His imminent Cross to save us from eternal tears, Jesus Himself was reduced to tears:- *In the days of His flesh Jesus offered up prayers and supplications, with loud cries and tears to Him Who was able to save Him from death."* (Hebrews 5:7) His tears were not in vain. His tears resulted in triumph. His pain leads to our Paradise - a home in glory forevermore, *an inheritance which is imperishable, undefiled, and unfading,* (1 Peter 1:4)

So, because of the Cross of Jesus, we may take heart if we are Christians, that one day, we will cry no more as *He will wipe away every tear from their eyes, and death will be no more, neither shall there be mourning nor crying nor pain anymore, for the former things have passed away.* (Revelation 21:4)

> *Our God has fixed the happy day*
> *When the last tear shall dim our eyes*
> *When He will wipe all tears away*
> *And fill our hearts with glad surprise*
> *To hear His voice to see His face*
> *And know the riches of His grace.*

Soli Deo Gloria

THE LIGHT OF HEAVEN IS THE FACE OF
JESUS,

THE JOY OF HEAVEN IS THE PRESENCE
OF JESUS,

THE MELODY OF HEAVEN IS THE
NAME OF JESUS,

THE HARMONY OF HEAVEN IS THE
PRAISE OF JESUS,

THE THEME OF HEAVEN IS THE WORK
OF JESUS,

THE EMPLOYMENT OF HEAVEN IS THE
SERVICE OF JESUS,

THE FULLNESS OF HEAVEN IS JESUS
HIMSELF!

How bright these glorious spirits shine!
Whence all their bright array?
How came they to the blissful seats
of everlasting day?

Lo! these are they from sufferings great,
Who came to realms of light;
And in the blood of Christ have washed
Those robes that shine so bright.

Now with triumphant palms they stand
Before the throne on high
And serve the God they love, amidst
The glories of the sky

Hunger and thirst are felt no more,
Nor suns with scorching ray;
God is their Sun, whose cheering beams
Diffuse the eternal day.

The Lamb, Who dwells amidst the throne,
Shall oe'r them still preside,
Feed them with nourishment divine
And all their footsteps guide.

'Midst pastures green He'll lead His flock
Where living streams appear;
And God the Lord from every eye
Shall wipe away each tear.

To Father, Son and Holy Ghost,
The God Whom we adore,
Be glory, as it was is now
And shall be evermore.

Based on Revelation 7: 13-17